Why Change Is Hard

Why Change Is Hard

*The Power of Master Narratives
Over Self and Society*

KATE C. McLEAN

Oxford University Press is a department of the University of Oxford. It furthers
the University's objective of excellence in research, scholarship, and education
by publishing worldwide. Oxford is a registered trade mark of Oxford University
Press in the UK and certain other countries.

Published in the United States of America by Oxford University Press
198 Madison Avenue, New York, NY 10016, United States of America.

© Kate C. McLean 2024

All rights reserved. No part of this publication may be reproduced, stored in
a retrieval system, or transmitted, in any form or by any means, without the
prior permission in writing of Oxford University Press, or as expressly permitted
by law, by license, or under terms agreed with the appropriate reproduction
rights organization. Inquiries concerning reproduction outside the scope of the
above should be sent to the Rights Department, Oxford University Press, at the
address above.

You must not circulate this work in any other form
and you must impose this same condition on any acquirer.

Library of Congress Cataloging-in-Publication Data
Names: McLean, Kate C., author.
Title: Why change is hard : the power of master narratives over self and society / Kate C. McLean.
Description: New York, NY : Oxford University Press, [2024] |
Includes bibliographical references and index. |
Identifiers: LCCN 2023043027 (print) | LCCN 2023043028 (ebook) |
ISBN 9780197764640 (hardback) | ISBN 9780197764664 (epub) |
ISBN 9780197764671
Subjects: LCSH: Change (Psychology) | Social change.
Classification: LCC BF637.C4 M35 2024 (print) | LCC BF637.C4 (ebook) |
DDC 158.1—dc23/eng/20231120
LC record available at https://lccn.loc.gov/2023043027
LC ebook record available at https://lccn.loc.gov/2023043028

DOI: 10.1093/oso/9780197764640.001.0001

Printed by Integrated Books International, United States of America

This book is dedicated to my dad, John Bolen Carter, who taught me about the power of systems and structures, the power of resistance, and the power of stories.

CONTENTS

Acknowledgments ix

Part I: Laying the Foundations: History, Culture, and Theories

1. Introduction: Time for a Change 3

2. Foundations: Culture and History 19

3. Theoretical Foundations: Identities, Stories, and Change 37

Part II: The Data on Change

4. Evidence for Change From the Field of Personality Development: Traits, Attachment, and Posttraumatic Growth 65

5. Evidence for Change in Narrative Identity: The Case of Repeated Narration 77

Part III: Special Concerns

6. Transgressions as an Opportunity for Change? 97

7. The Agency in Resistance 110

Part IV: Conclusion

8. Our Scientific Responsibility for Change 131

References 141
Index 165

ACKNOWLEDGMENTS

Thank you to Moin Syed who provided feedback on selected chapters, told me to do something "weird" when I really needed to hear that, and for being a general partner in crime for years. Thank you to Onnie Rogers who provided feedback on selected chapters, for giving me critical and important feedback, and for engaging in vibrant in-person and email conversations about these issues; her thinking and feedback have been particularly important for how I understand agency and resistance. Thank you to Monisha Pasupathi who challenged me in her typical gracious and supportive way, always helping me to realize what I was missing. Thank you to Brianna Delker who engaged in a book club series about trauma and change, who provided feedback on selected chapters, and served as a sounding board throughout the process. Thank you to Jennifer Texas Tackett who provided feedback on selected chapters, encouraged me to read Jung (and read some with me), helped me to apply the ideas to real life, and reminded me about grieving the story when (and if) it changes. Thank you to Adam Sinton who sent me podcasts to listen to and was always ready to dig into the ideas. Thank you to my friends who cheered me along the way and distracted me when needed: Karen Cohen, Annie Riggs, Annie Fast, Heather Whitaker, Jen Stephens, and Anna Ciao. Thank you to Peter Lewis Webster Jones who helped me to refine the ocean liner metaphor for two degrees of change in Chapter 5.

I have also had some structured opportunities to play with these ideas. I was lucky enough to teach several seminars on identity change, and I was gifted with wonderful students who dug into these ideas with enthusiasm. I was grateful to give talks at the Society for Applied Research in Memory and Cognition, Northwestern University, and the University of California, Santa Cruz, as I was developing these ideas. And I am grateful to Western Washington University for supporting my research and my year of sabbatical during which I wrote this book.

Finally, this book started as so many of my projects do, over conversations with Lewis Webster Jones. And it ended with him as well—the best editor I could ask for. I continue to be surprised, delighted, and deeply grateful to have found a partner who simultaneously supports and challenges my thinking and my work.

PART I

Laying the Foundations

History, Culture, and Theories

1

Introduction

Time for a Change

It is perhaps the most dominant message in mainstream American culture: that individuals, alone and by sheer force of will, have the power to control their own destinies.

> The greatest discovery of all time is that a person can change his future by merely changing his attitude.
> —Oprah Winfrey

> We can change our lives. We can do, have, and be exactly what we wish.
> —Tony Robbins

> Realize that you are the only thing stopping you.
> —Richard Branson

The idea that we are the only thing standing in our way—that positive personal change is always within reach, that change is equally available to everyone, as long as they are willing to work hard—is such a pervasive message, so taken for granted in our popular culture, that it's really more than just an idea; it's a *belief*. Adopt the right personal habits, the right diet, the right life hacks . . . and the change you desire will surely be yours.

Why Change Is Hard. Kate C. McLean, Oxford University Press. © Kate C. McLean 2024.
DOI: 10.1093/oso/9780197764640.003.0001

But this is not just a contemporary ideology espoused by celebrities and employed as a mass marketing strategy. This assumption of boundless agency and autonomy and the possibility—the *promise*—of change, if you have the strength of character to seize it, runs deep. It is rooted in the country's most foundational texts—legal, religious, and philosophical—texts that helped to create the systems and structures in which Americans live. Take the Constitution, which emphasizes the possibility of growth toward a more perfect union alongside the enshrinement of individual rights that will get us there. Or the Bible, with its emphasis on the possibility of personal redemption, suggesting a storyline for personal change (see McAdams, 2006). Manifest Destiny was declared as part of the "natural rights of man" to expand into and dominate North America (O'Sullivan, 1845). And the notion of the self-made man permeated American society from its earliest beginnings (see de Tocqueville, 1835).

With this emphasis on the unique power of the individual, it almost seems as if there is no context, culture, structure, or system in which this hyperautonomous person is living. With enough determination, with enough grit, you can become whoever and whatever you want.

Given the ubiquity of this assumption, it should come as no surprise that the radical individualism that runs rampant in mainstream American culture also permeates the field of psychology, my home turf. Indeed, it is not only Oprah who espouses the promise of change.

> What is necessary to change a person is to change his awareness of himself.
>
> —Abraham Maslow

> Between stimulus and response there is a space. In that space is our power to choose our response. In our response lies our growth and our freedom.
>
> —Viktor E. Frankl

The idea that we have the power to change our mindsets, that we can change our orientation toward relationships, our traits and self-views, the idea that we can transform through and after adversity, that we are the authors of the stories we tell—these ideas are the bedrock of our modern psychological science. When we humans run into trouble, are unsatisfied, unhappy, or stuck, we can change our situations, our lives, our selves. We can simply eat more vegetables, do more sit-ups, wake up earlier. We can go to therapy or change our medication or download a meditation app. *Realize that you are the only thing stopping you.* What power we have.

These messages about the power of the individual are transmitted through *master narratives*, shared cultural stories that guide the construction of our personal stories (Hammack, 2008; McLean & Syed, 2015; Syed & McLean, 2021a). Master narratives about the power of the individual center on tales of persevering through challenge, overcoming the odds, and reaching new heights. These are stories that inspire us and guide us. Stories that are useful to us, that serve particular ends, such as conveying values, instructing us on how to live a good life, and providing a template to organize our experiences. They help us to learn about our culture, our history, our traditions. And when our personal stories align with these master narratives, we feel validated, seen; we feel connected to others, part of a community with shared values, shared history, and common ground.

But there is a dark side to master narratives. They are not simply benign reflections of values, a scaffold to organize our own experiences into a story, and a means of building community connections. Master narratives represent a very *particular* story, and it is never the full story. They represent *a* history, *a* set of values. And the particular values and history that are represented in master narratives serve to maintain hierarchies of power that benefit those at the top (McLean & Syed, 2015; Syed & McLean, 2021a, 2022). Put bluntly, master narratives uphold systems of power and privilege. The press of how to tell the *right* story, and how to lead the *right* life inherent in master narratives, uplifts values that maintain an inequitable status quo. That story about the power of the individual—that she can change herself, by herself—excludes the systems in which that person lives, systems that may thwart her power, that may be *designed* to thwart her power.

Although master narratives are the most dominant and dangerously powerful stories, these are not the only stories we have. We also have *alternative* narratives. These narratives rely on another version of the past; they give us a different story that does not work to uphold the status quo, but that challenges the status quo, that even resists the status quo (Rogers & Way, 2018, 2021).

When we consider the founding ideologies and narratives of the United States from a master narrative approach, the distinction between master and alternative narratives is clear. Depending on who we're listening to, we get wildly different stories. One story, the master narrative, is that the country was built on the resilience and grit of courageous individuals who pulled themselves up by their bootstraps, toiling through adversity to triumph. This upward movement was a divine right toward progress—Manifest Destiny. These inspirational stories of triumph instill in us the idea that anything is possible. If we can just work hard enough, we too can conquer that which seeks to stop us. The possibilities are endless in the land of the free. The values in these origin myths made their way into our founding documents, ensuring life, liberty, and happiness through the independence and the rights of the individual. These are the messages that infuse our culture still. But this master narrative of the origin of this country belies a much more treacherous and oppressive set of ideologies and stories on which the United States was *also* founded.

If we zoom out from the myopic focus on this powerful individual surmounting all odds, we see something else. We see the context in which that individual is situated. We see an origin myth that begins with a land that was not free to be taken; it was not empty, full of possibility and room for growth. We see a people for whom this land was already home, from whom we stole this land. In this story, Manifest Destiny was not divinely ordained but was a human-made, self-serving idea that was used to systematically justify mass murder and the stealing of lands for profit and power, to benefit a race of people who thought themselves superior. We see a country founded on the enslavement of other human beings for profit and power. We see a context in which particular individuals created a structure and a system in which they alone would thrive. We see that they enshrined "individual rights" in the Constitution, but only for some. We see that they defined enslaved people as not full human beings. We see that they gave a select few these lauded "individual rights" that we hold up with such awe; these rights were given only to white,[1] property-owning men.

Using this alternative frame of analysis, it is not individual hard work that is most notable; it is instead the collective effort to build a system *designed for* the privileged few. White Christian men strategically built a structure in which they alone would thrive and dominate. They created laws, tax systems, and societal machinery to benefit themselves and to deny access to others. "[W]hite men have benefitted from their own affirmative action programs for hundreds of years since the inception of this country" (Spencer, 2017, p. 307). And yet the master narrative is one in which *individuals* are construed as solely responsible for their success. But it is a success that was made possible by the *structure* they built, by the *system* that they made to benefit them.

The argument that I want to make in this book is that if we don't see master narratives as powerful structures that uphold inequitable and oppressive systems, we will continue to perpetuate harm. Not understanding the power of master narratives actually stymies the possibility of progress and change. If we don't see the master narrative of personal responsibility for growth and change as rooted in white supremacy and patriarchy, this narrative will continue to thrive.

In making this argument about the harmful ideology of personal responsibility for change, I will draw from my research on identity development, and personality development more broadly. As I have worked through the literature, I have seen how my discipline, and my own work, has been based on this ideology of the possibility for change, and the individual responsibility for that change. And it has been both illuminating and distressing to realize that the data we have are not always very

---

1. I am intentionally not capitalizing "white" because of the historical and current connection, between the capitalized form of the word and white supremacist organizations and thinking, and in solidarity with scholarship on anti-racism (see Hawkman, 2020).

good. I think psychologists, like everyone else, have absorbed this ideology, letting this master narrative about the power of the individual go unchallenged.

PERSONAL CHANGE AND THE STUDY OF STORIES

When psychologists think about change, we are often thinking about things like changing people's behavior, their personality traits, their relationship style, or—what I am most interested in—changing their stories, the way they interpret their past experiences. My primary focus is on the stories we tell about ourselves, stories that constitute our narrative identities. Humans are natural storytellers. We tell stories all the time, often with ourselves as the central character. This storytelling serves many important human needs, including figuring out who we are and communicating that identity to other people. In childhood and adolescence, kids can begin to tell stories that explain who they are—why they love to draw, why they want to be a teacher or an astronaut, why they're shy in groups, how their anxieties ebb and flow with family conflict. We learn to understand these parts of ourselves and how they fit together through the stories we tell about ourselves (e.g., Fivush, 2019).

Not surprisingly, given the sociohistorical foundation I just presented, this developmental process is viewed as a fairly individualistic one. To be sure, there is a lot of work on the sociocultural context of *early* narrative development, particularly on the role parents play in helping kids to learn *how* to tell stories (e.g., Nelson & Fivush, 2004). But once we get to be serviceable storytellers—sometime in the teen years—the storyteller is often presumed to take the reins and construct her own narrative about herself. This presumption is, of course, rooted in the individualistic culture in which most research participants and scientists studying storytelling are living.

The problem is that this is not how it works. The stories we tell about ourselves are not constructed on our own (e.g., Fivush, 2019; McLean, 2015; McLean & Syed, 2015; Merrill & Fivush, 2016; Pasupathi, 2001; Thorne,

2000). Our stories are guided by cultural and interpersonal expectations for how stories should be told. And yet we still think we have control over our stories. At least that's what we want to believe. That's what we're told to believe by cultural figures, media, and foundational texts. And quite honestly that's the case we make as scientists, even when the data suggest some important caveats to that idea.

But when you seriously consider the sociocultural context in which identities are built, you have to question the degree of this agency in storytelling (McLean & Syed, 2015; Syed & McLean, 2021a). If you think cultural expectations are real, that they matter, then you have to see that they don't merely provide a scaffold but also constrain and restrict the stories we tell. You have to see that master narratives tell us not only what stories to tell and how to tell them; they also let us know what stories are *not* to be told. When we look at master narratives in this light, we see that "agency is a powerful psychological resource, but we do a disservice to the reality of individual experience by not accounting for the structures that limit agency" (McLean & Syed, 2015, p. 326).

To be clear, it is not that I think we have *no* agency in authoring ourselves. It is that we, as a culture and as a discipline, have *overemphasized* personal control and agency so much that we are blinded to the limits of that agency. If we don't understand those limits, we will assume that the ability to change solely through personal autonomy is possible when it is not. And when people don't change their lives and their stories, we will blame them. We will not understand the role that larger structures and systems play in individual lives, and thus will be unmotivated to change the structures and systems that constrain stories and selves.

Moving From Persons to Systems and Structure

This book actually began when I started writing my first book on the *coauthored self* (McLean, 2015). In that book I made the argument that as we are beginning to define our identities, in adolescence, others define our story more than we might think. You can think of families as a mini-culture, with their own local master narratives (our family stories) that scaffold and constrain us. In fact, our families have an outsize influence not only in helping us to construct the stories we tell but also in the stories they tell about us. Like the story that your mom keeps telling about how you crashed the car when you were 16, and how she still doesn't want to drive with you. Or the narrative that you are the "emotional one" in the family, and each time you express an opinion it's just further evidence of your emotional volatility. Even if we disagree with those evaluations, we have to negotiate with them. Even as we resist them, they mark us. So the limit of agency here is that we can't control *others'* stories, and those other stories are a part of our identities, like it or not.

I wrote that book on the coauthored self in Santa Cruz, California, on the first sabbatical I had as a professor. On one of the first days of sabbatical, before I had barely written a word, I was walking along West Cliff Drive with my husband, and he said, "But wait . . . you're gonna have to address the question of whether people can *change* their stories. That's what people want to know about." I quickly put the kibosh on that—I had a book to write and it was not about change. I wasn't interested in the Secret to Changing Your Story in Seven Steps. And I'm still not. I'll leave that to the Tony Robbinses of the world.

But I did start to ponder the question. How *do* people change? *Do* people actually change? When I ask myself and others the question: "Can people change?" the answer comes quickly, easily. Yes, of course, people *can* change. But when I ask: *Do* people change? . . . things get a little quiet. Early in this process I told a friend of mine I was working on a book with the working title *Can You Change Your Story?* Let me save you a lot of time. He said: No.

So then the question becomes: Why? Why is it so hard to change? Why do so few people undergo fundamental, identity-altering change? What's the deal?!

As I have mulled over these ideas, started to get deeper into various literatures about change, had more conversations than I can count, taught courses on the topic, and, yes, listened to a lot of podcasts, my frame of analysis was also changing. My initial frame, part of my academic origin story, begins with my advisor, Avril Thorne. Avril is, among her cohort, wonderful and weird. She is a personality psychologist, part of a group of people who primarily focus on internal and intrapsychic aspects of persons. Avril was interested in narrative identity, the stories we tell about ourselves. But she was more interested in the *telling* part than her compatriots. What happens when we share our stories with others? How do their responses and reactions shape the story? She was challenging the idea that our stories are internalized representations, relatively untouched by the cultures and contexts in which we live.

That frame made a big impact on me. Although I spent most of the first chunk of my career working on the idea of autobiographical reasoning, on how *individuals* make meaning of important past events, the social context of that reasoning always seemed to sneak into my analyses. Over time that social context crept more and more centrally into my thinking. As my confidence expanded and my freedom to explore different ideas grew with the securities that come with things like getting a job and tenure, I started to put context more squarely at the center of my thinking, focusing for some time on interpersonal contexts of storytelling and identity-making, like families. I became more deeply impacted by other scholars who were finding creative and thoughtful ways to push the field toward a more contextual analysis. People like Monisha Pasupathi (e.g., 2001), Robyn Fivush (e.g., Fivush & Reese, 2002), and Phil Hammack (e.g., 2008) who were pushing boundaries around identity and the sociocultural contexts in which it develops, people who were doing work that inspired me and encouraged me to venture down different paths than the mainstream of my field.

In more recent years, I have worked with my colleagues on the larger cultural and structural context of storytelling, and less on interpersonal contexts like families. I see a similarity in the way stories told by our close others define us, and the way that cultural stories define us. With my friend and 7th cousin, Moin Syed, I also started working on ideas about how culture itself is maintained, and how it possibly changes, through storytelling (McLean & Syed, 2015). As I moved down this pathway, I found

I could not disentangle culture and the structures and systems of a society from the individual. And now, any time I hear a personal story, I also hear a story of a system, of a culture; I hear a story about the structure of the world in which we are building and telling our stories.

Another scholar who has been deeply influential in encouraging me down some new paths is Onnie Rogers. She makes the argument that we cannot answer the classic identity question, "Who am I?" without also asking, "Who are we?" (Rogers, 2020). She makes this argument based on her interviews with kids who connect these two dots between the I and the we quite naturally, often kids who have been placed on the margins of society in the United States. These kids know that their identities are defined by the worlds in which they live, defined not only by the stories they tell, but also by the stories told about them. Rogers and Way (2018) quote a 14-year-old Black boy they call Devin:

> I'm just glad to be Black you know, even though there's like a lot of stereotypes . . . like, Black men really don't like to grow up, either they're like drug dealers or gang bangers, or end up dead or something like that, or end up in jail. (p. 13)

Like other youth, Devin is in no small part defined by these cultural stories about what it means to be a Black man. These stories cannot be ignored. And Devin chooses to resist them:

> No, since I'm Black I feel like I gotta, you know, achieve somethin' other than that, you know? I've got goals to do. Like they say Black men probably won't make it, but I know I'm going to make it and even if I don't make it, I'll still try to do something. I just can't—it's not me, I just can't be nothin'; I've got to do something. (p. 13)

This resistance is a powerful form of agency (see also Rogers & Way, 2021; Chapter 7). But it is not all-powerful agency. Even in the strength of his resistance, Devin has to contend with these stories. He is not an agent of radical autonomy, outside of any structure or system. He is smack in the middle of it. If he wants to change the story about himself, he has to contend with these systems of power (Rogers & Way, 2021).

But my argument is not just about those on the margins. When it comes to defining ourselves, we *all* have limits to our agency. These systems are also a part of the identities of Devin's white friends who are privileged by virtue of their skin color. It is just easier to ignore how much systems shape our identities from particular positions of power and privilege.[2] But when we take a truly cultural, structural, and systemic approach to the study of identity, we have to contend with the way that systems and structures define us all, and the collective responsibility we have for changing them.

The way power emerges in my work is in my focus on master narratives, like the master narrative about the individual agency to change, which is derived in part from a colonial history that intentionally upheld white supremacy and patriarchy. I view these shared cultural stories as structures that maintain the status quo that benefits those privileged by virtue of race, gender, and wealth, among other attributes. These stories help to maintain traditional power hierarchies. When we hold on to the idea that we are solely in control of our own narratives, we maintain systems that benefit those with privileged lives.

Understanding the power of these stories may be as simple as where we "start" the story, because that determines its course (Adichie, 2009). In my brief (and rudimentary) analysis of the country's founding, I started at two different points. The master narrative starts with the battle for liberation from England. The alternative narrative starts with the people who were

---

2. This brings to mind how the crack cocaine crisis of the 1980s and 1990s was viewed versus the more recent opioid crisis (see Equal Justice Initiative, 2019). It appears that there is a shift in how we assign blame (poor choices vs. disease) and how we respond (prison vs. treatment). The move toward fewer legal consequence and more awareness of addiction as a disease comes with an awareness of the *systems* in which these processes are occurring, such as the role of pharmaceutical companies, federal regulatory bodies, and health care entities in the facilitation of drug abuse. And isn't it interesting that this shift toward an awareness of the limits of personal responsibility happened when white communities were more noticeably impacted by addiction? In other words, the status quo was no longer acceptable once the privileged were impacted.

here before the battle. Where we start the story determines its course and the lessons we take from it. For example:

> When we start the story with the *criminal*, we miss the systems of systemic oppression in which that *person* was born into (Alexander, 2010).
>
> When we start the story with victims and survivors of sexual violence, we miss the patriarchy that has maintained systems of gender-based power for millennia (e.g., Delker, Salton, & McLean, 2020).
>
> When we start the story with the individual's successful battle with cancer, we miss the health care system that allows early detection for those more structurally privileged (e.g., Yee, Mazumder, Dong, & Neeki, 2020).

Not starting with context and history, or removing it all together, means that we tell an entirely different story—a story that features the protagonist rather than the context.

Some may say, "But we're psychologists—we focus on people!" And, yes, we do. But people are not separate from their context (e.g., Cikara, Martinez, & Lewis, 2022; Crossing, Gumudavelly, Watkins, Logue, & Anderson, 2022; Fish & Syed, 2018; Garcia-Coll et al., 1996; Rogers, Niwa Chung, Yip, & Chae, 2021; Rogers & Way, 2021; Rogoff, 2003; Settles, Warner, Buchanan, & Jones, 2020; Spencer, 2017; Spencer, Dupree, & Hartmann, 1997). We *cannot* understand people—their behaviors, their thoughts, their emotions, their stories, and their identities—if we don't understand the context that they are in. It is like going to the doctor for back pain, and she only looks at your back. Not your pronated feet, or your ankle injury, or the impact of caring for an infant or an aging parent.

I recently read an article in which the authors argued that to address systemic inequality we need to study exceptions—those people who rise out of poverty or overcome other adversity to achieve a kind of success (the people who follow the master narrative) (Ruggeri & Folke, 2022). Once we learn how such people make this herculean effort, we can then create interventions to assist others in doing that work. Really? No attention to the obstacles in the way? How to change *those*? No analysis of what is wrong with the system we are asking people to conform to? Instead, we'll just task those already under incredible stress, those "experiencing adversity," with solving the problem by being superheroes.

And such an approach may cause harm. For example, Miller, Chen, and Brody (2015) looked at those "exceptional" kids as well. They found that after experiencing an intervention to improve "character skills" like self-control, some youth who were highly structurally disadvantaged—who were not supposed to succeed—did. For some of these youth, this training in self-control resulted in good things over time, like succeeding in school and experiencing less depression and substance use. But don't start the individual intervention celebration just yet. These interventions *also* predicted poor health outcomes, *but only for those who came from families with less money*. These youth experienced more rapid physiological aging over time. And the exact opposite was true for wealthier youth: the interventions were positive all around. What this says to me is that adjusting to a maladjusted world, conforming to a society that systemically oppresses you, comes with real-world consequences that we often do not want to see (see also Hamblin, 2015; Rogers & Heard-Garris, 2023; Rogers & Way, 2018).

Again, to be clear, I am not fully knocking the study of individual characteristics, and the importance of traits or resilience, because they are important. Resilience is powerful. And I am not only knocking others' research programs. My own research is definitely implicated here. What I am saying is that we need to change our frame. We need to start thinking structurally. It's time to stop studying and uplifting the exceptions. Because exceptions are just that: *exceptions*. It's time to start studying the rule.

SCIENTIFIC RESPONSIBILITY FOR CHANGE

The problem regarding which narratives we privilege, and which we deny and dismiss, is a systemic problem. It is a problem supported by our capitalist and neoliberal systems (e.g., Kasser, Cohn, Kanner, & Ryan, 2007). In such systems, a collective and contextual frame undermines the bottom line of economic growth. I'm not an economist, but it seems that the economic and regulatory structures we have built are guided by master narratives of individual grit and personal responsibility, of the power of the individual to overcome odds, even as they provide a *structural* benefit for the privileged. We expect people to work hard to make money, which we view as a sign of character and resilience, yet we have structures that allow the wealthy to *not* work as their generational wealth accumulates, relatively untaxed. Gill and Orgad (2018) argue that the focus on resilience is

> part of a broader "turn to character" (Bull and Allen, 2018) in contemporary capitalism, that has been especially evident in policy discourses.... [R]esilience sits alongside other notions such as confidence, creativity, and entrepreneurialism, as being among the key qualities and dispositions highlighted as necessary to survive and thrive in neoliberal societies. We see the promotion of resilience as part of an increasingly *psychological turn* within neoliberalism, intensified by austerity, in which new ways of being, relating, and apprehending the self are produced. (p. 478)

This problem of focusing on the individual can be seen not only in our economic infrastructure but also in many other domains. And the reach of that ideology makes it that much more intractable. But as widespread as these concerns are, we have to start somewhere, and I am drawing special attention to the problem that I and my colleagues have. Although the premise of our modern science rests on the idea that scientists are unbiased observers of the Truth, the field of psychology is not immune or exempt from, or unaffected by, the larger culture. We do not sit outside culture. We are in it. We are part of it. And we are responsible for some of these messages.

We have *helped* the engineers of the marketplace with this "psychological turn" that fosters systems that benefit the wealthy. We have primarily upheld master narratives, and many of us have dismissed alternative narratives. Most of us have paid too little attention to structures and systems. Perhaps this is because scientists are also people who are embedded in these systems. And many of us are in positions of privilege that make it easier to ignore these systems. But psychologists should know better than most that we are not unbiased observers. We are impacted by the architecture of society as much as anyone. And so we too (over)value stories about the power of the individual.

And let's not forget that many of us also have stories about hard work that are personally meaningful. Think of all the work it took to get into and through college, to gain entry into a PhD program and make it through, to secure a job in academia and to earn tenure. All of those achievements took a lot of hard work. They involved late nights of study and writing, endless practice talks and oral defenses, persevering through journal rejection after rejection, and sacrificing time with family or time to do anything else. All of this involved individual hard work. But we all know *we did not do it alone.* Perhaps we had truly supportive mentors, a cohort of other students with whom to commiserate, and families who encouraged us. And, of course, we had *systems* of support—grants, loans, university health insurance, and structured mentoring programs. I do not mean to say that these systems are perfect, or that they are equitable in who they support and uplift. Nor do I mean to discount the late nights or individual efforts. I only mean to bring our attention to the systems that support some and exclude others.

Although I think that my field has contributed important knowledge toward understanding the human condition, I also think we are at a crossroads. We are at a moment in which we need to engage in the kind of reflective analysis we encourage in others. There is a reckoning in psychology right now—critiques of our scientific practices (e.g., Nosek, 2014; Spellman, 2015; Yarkoni, 2022), of our lack of diversity and inclusivity (e.g., Roberts, Bareket-Shavit, Dollins, Goldie, & Mortenson, 2020; Syed & Kathawalla, 2021), of the ways we have perpetuated harm and trauma in particular domains (Delker, 2021; Rogers, in press) and for particular people (Fish & Syed, 2018). So when we talk about many of the things psychologists study—personal well-being, posttraumatic growth, personal identity, and so on—without acknowledging the role that culture, structures, and systems play in understanding whether someone is psychologically well-adjusted, we are part of the problem.

The call in this book is one of a growing chorus to step back and consider what we are doing, the impact it has, and how we can, and must, do better (Crossing et al., 2022; Fish, 2022; Fox & Fine, 2013; Ledgerwood et al., 2022; Lewis, 2021; Roberts, Bareket-Shavit, Dollins, Goldie, & Mortenson, 2020; Rogers, Moffitt, McLean, & Syed, 2023; Rogers & Way, 2021; Salter & Adams, 2013; Settles, Warner, Buchanan, & Jones, 2020; Spencer, 2017; Teo, 2010). We need to understand our own complicity in creating the cultural practices we study and in upholding systems of oppression and inequity (Cushman, 1996; see also Adams, Estrada-Villalta, Sullivan, & Markus, 2019; Rogers et al., 2023). If, as a field, we continue to focus primarily on the characteristics of the individual in understanding their functioning or success, we are complicit in the lack of systemic change.

Through my work on this book, I have come to the conclusion that change—both for the person and the society—is probably very, very hard. And one of the major reasons that change is so hard is that it is *not* under the sole authority of the individual. This hyperfocused spotlight on the person allows us to ignore, even to deny, the importance of context, culture, structures, and systems. When we deny and ignore the architecture of society, we perpetuate harmful stories. And one of those harmful stories is about the personal responsibility for change.

Those who know me know that I am an optimist, perhaps even overly positive and enthusiastic at times. I'm no Debbie Downer. But, like many, I have become so frustrated with my scientific community, with the culture at large, with the way we do things and *keep* doing things, reifying and reinforcing the same old status quo, that my goal is to make an argument about the challenge of change in the hopes of actually making some change. Because I *am* an optimist. I do believe that change is *possible*. But I am also a realist. And we can only change if we truly understand what we are up against and the role we play in the maintenance of the status quo.

2

Foundations

Culture and History

Given the foundation I established in Chapter 1, as we begin to look at what makes change so difficult, we are not going to begin with the almighty individual, who gets plenty of attention already, that person who is literally at the center of our usual analyses and theoretical frameworks (e.g., Bronfenbrenner, 1979). Instead, I want to begin this book where some of my colleagues have recently argued is a more appropriate starting point for understanding individual development—with the cultural and historical context. As I've said, but it bears repeating, we simply can't understand a person's identity without understanding the context in which that person lives (e.g., Fish & Syed, 2018; Rogers, Niwa, Chung, Yip, & Chae, 2021; see also Garcia-Coll et al., 1996; Lerner, 2006; Spencer, Dupree, & Hartmann, 1997; Spencer, 2017; Weisner, 2002).

As I have articulated, my central thesis is that a hyperfocus on the self allows us to disregard the sociohistorical context and the systems and structures of society in which the individual develops. And this disregard leads to a flawed idea about the power individuals possess to change their lives at will. In this chapter I will examine how systems and individuals are connected from some different vantage points, by looking at movements to understand and dismantle systemic racism, as well as examining the study of posttraumatic growth. And I will also interrogate the role of the discipline of psychology in perpetuating an imbalance in the disproportionate attention to self over society.

And a note... when I use the terms "we" and "our," I mean mainstream American culture. In using the term "mainstream," I intend to target the dominant and powerful aspects of culture that are entrenched in our laws, systems, and most perceptible, noisiest values. I am not talking about the substantial diversity, variations, and subcultures within the United States, but about the parts of our culture with which we must all deal and negotiate, even if they do not represent our own lives and values. I am talking about the master narratives that dictate what it means to be a good person and how to lead a good life in this culture—the narratives that dictate how to story our experiences and what stories we should tell and not tell. Even if we resist and reject these master narratives, we are still in negotiation with them through our acts of resistance.

CULTURE: DEFINITIONS, POWER, AND THE STATUS QUO

I define culture as a set of *valued practices* that help people to understand how to be a member of a community. Practices are what people actually *do*. These practices run from the relatively everyday and benign—like reading to children before bed, calling elders by their first name, standing during the national anthem before a baseball game—to practices of much greater consequence like prescribing pain medication to certain patients and not others, or enacting laws that restrict or allow access to abortion. And storytelling is an everyday practice that can be both benign and of great consequence.

And these things that people do—the foods they eat, the stories they tell, the laws they pass—represent particular *values*. These things we do represent the things that are important to us.[1] Knowing what's important

---

1. The things we *don't* do likewise tell us about what is important to us. For example, the United States does not have structural support for raising children, such as paid family leave for all, affordable or free day care, or universal pre-kindergarten. What does that tell us about our values?

means that we know what's expected and thus we know how to be a member of our group or, more specifically, how to be a *good* member of our group. And when we engage in these expected behaviors, we help to maintain and perpetuate that culture.

This Vygotskian definition that I use in my research comes from the study of the cultural nature of human development and how the dynamic participation of community members in these practices makes up a culture (e.g., Rogoff, 2003; Weisner, 2002). This is in contrast to more traditional and mainstream conceptions of culture like individualism and collectivism, which, although they also define culture as sets of behaviors, values, and ways of thinking, are terms that are usually employed as independent variables that "cause" behavior (e.g., Markus & Kitayama, 1991; see also Syed & Kathawalla, 2018). That is, culture is typically thought of as influencing people in a relatively static, top-down manner; it is a way of defining culture that doesn't tell me about what people actually do or their role in perpetuating culture.

Such traditional approaches also do not illuminate how individuals negotiate with their culture: how they live in it, understand it, and how they feel a sense of belonging to or exclusion from it. This is where I find it useful to integrate the master narrative approach with a Vygotskian approach, because the master narrative approach does not view culture as value-neutral. Our expectations, even requirements, for how to live in our communities favor particular practices or activities, such as marriage or standing for the national anthem. That's fine for those who like those practices or who can easily and comfortably engage in them. Not so much for those who don't. From this perspective, cultures can have some pretty rigid boundaries with sanctions for those who cross them.

However, even with this rigidity, I still think of culture as dynamic because of my focus on activity. Culture is about people doing things, and the activities they engage in sustain it. Culture is not just a top-down behemoth directing our every move. We are players in the game of creating, sustaining, and *potentially* changing culture. But, in practice, it's true that we do a lot of sustaining.

The Rigidity of Culture and the Challenge of Change

Although we can put a simple tagline on cultural values—"Hard work will be rewarded"—these values really come to life and are best transmitted through stories. Saying you should work hard is much more understandable, and convincing, when it comes in the form of a story, like a Horatio Alger narrative in which the hard work of the protagonist pays off with success and achievement. Moin Syed and I have argued that culture is developed, sustained, and perhaps changed through the transmission of particular stories: *cultural master narratives* (McLean & Syed, 2015; Syed & McLean, 2021a; see also Hammack 2008). These master narratives provide guidance for telling stories and constructing the self in ways that facilitate being a good member of one's community. They also facilitate the *maintenance* of the status quo, the culture as is.

In fact, my work with Moin focuses a good deal on the *constraints* of cultural stories for individual lives. The directives inherent in these stories mean that there is the possibility of not aligning with expectations. For those who don't fit the bill, these master narratives can exclude, shame, and deny membership or community participation. And these narratives are most likely to deny inclusion to those who are the most disempowered, least privileged, or least likely to benefit from the status quo. Those in power tend to like power and want to maintain their position in the hierarchy. And one way to do that is to perpetuate particular stories to maintain an inequitable status quo that benefits those in power.

One of the clearest examples of how stories can be used to maintain hierarchies of power is in the context of systemic American racism. A master narrative in the United States asserts that when it comes to race relations and racism, there has been profound progress made over time (so much so that some are arguing that the Voting Rights Act and affirmative action policies are no longer needed). Moving from enslavement to a Black president is, for many, the ultimate redemption. And it is a popular story, seen in Hollywood movies such as *Green Book*, *42*, and *The Butler*, to name a few. These movies detail the pain and the struggle of racism, but they end with happiness and accomplishment (deep and lasting friendship, entry into the baseball hall of fame, seeing the first Black president inaugurated). For some—even for many—these stories are moving; they may even inspire those in the audience. It's hard to knock something that inspires. But one crux of my argument is that this inspiration comes at a cost, because the unhelpful master narrative about the immense power of individual effort leading to inevitable success gets packaged in such a sweet coating that it is too easy to ignore the flaws in the story.

Because, of course, this story is only one story. This story is a story of exception. This is not a story about the rule. It is not a story that represents the reality of our structures and systems. It is a story that puts racism in the rear view, as a part of history, not as a part of current systems. A much larger, more complicated story is about systems and *living* history. In other words, a focus on Jackie Robinson's success or Obama's electoral victory allows us to deny the system that makes them *exceptions*, inspirational as they may be. So the story of racial progress and American exceptionalism continues to be told, the practices that maintain systemic racism continue, and fundamental change is made more difficult (e.g., Richeson, 2020; Rucker & Richeson, 2021).

In an article for *The New York Review of Books*, historian and writer Jelani Cobb wrote about the ways our racist practices are sustained, despite prompts, nudges, even *warnings* about the need for change (Cobb, 2021; see also Delgado & Stafancic, 2000). He wrote about the Kerner Commission Report, which came out in 1968 (named for its Chair, Illinois Governor Otto Kerner). The report was commissioned by President Lyndon Johnson to examine "black anger over policing practices, voter suppression, poverty, and economic inequality," which had erupted in the early and mid-1960s in some American cities. Cobb wrote about the Kerner report 15 months after the uprisings in response to George Floyd's murder in 2020:

> the Kerner Report is instructive. "Our nation," it warned in 1968, "is moving toward two societies, one black, one white—separate and unequal." . . . After Floyd's death the media, lawmakers, and the public wondered how the nation had come to this. The Kerner

Report suggests that the more apt question should be why we have progressed so little beyond these combustible moments. The most recent incidents of state violence, the rioting in American streets, the often half-hearted scramble to understand the systemic failures and institutional rot that served as kindling for the latest conflagrations—*all seem like a grim recurrence of a chronic national predicament*. (emphasis in italics)

So how *did* we come to this? Repeated hand-wringing, commissions, eloquent speeches, marches, tears, anger. Indeed, Cobb writes that 6 years *before* Floyd's murder, in response to Michael Brown's murder:

> The Department of Justice conducted an investigation of the Ferguson Police Department and filed a report that could well have been an appendix to the Kerner Report. The recognition that policing was just one part of a broader systemic failure began to creep back into public recognition. And yet, scarcely six years later, the nation once again witnessed outrage in the streets. And yet, for all its [the report] strengths, it failed to discern that much of the American public had not the slightest appetite for such a form of liberalism.

No appetite. Which means people don't want to, or can't, hear the story about systemic and institutional racism in our country. Indeed, even when people are *explicitly reminded* of the persistence of inequality over time in American society, they perform all kinds of mental contortions to preserve their idea that we are better now. They contort their views of the past to preserve current belief systems that ignore these inequalities, preserving the narrative of progress (see Onyeador et al., 2020).

And these mental contortions that people perform to make themselves feel comfortable with the status quo are supported, are validated, by our structural architecture. *Right now*, laws are being placed on the books to systematically deny access to stories about slavery with the banning of the 1619 Project (Hannah-Jones, Roper, Silverman, & Silverstein, 2021). Books are being banned to systematically deny access to stories about and written by LGBTQ+ individuals and people of color (see Pen American, 2022). Although book banning often comes from community members, an unprecedented 41% of book bans over a 9-month period from July 2021 to March 2022 came from the directives of elected lawmakers or state officials. This is the system. This is the refusal to change, to *progress*, in real time, *right now*.

These systemic efforts have structural support—in our educational system (e.g., a lack of attention to the current legacy of slavery in textbooks; Southern Poverty Law Center, 2018), in the legal system (e.g., the money bail system; U.S. Commission on Civil Rights, 2022), and in media representations of the system working to get the bad guys (e.g., popular TV shows such as *Law and Order*; Andrews, 2022). Across these parts of our society, a story is promoted that puts American racism in the past and encourages a belief in the ability of the legal system to do justice. This story relieves us of our collective responsibility to change.

> The Kerner Commission had called the criminal justice system unjust, indicting racism for creating many of the troubles within black America. In the decade to come, this line of thinking was more likely to be attacked for leniency; it was supplanted by the view that racism had diminished and that black poverty was the product of bad choices, weak values, and lack of motivation. White society, exonerating itself from any culpability in the creation of a brutally segregated black America, now felt comfortable enough to offer judgment from afar. (Cobb, 2021)

The idea of personal responsibility as a cause of poverty is developed and perpetuated through political rhetoric and policies, and through stories that represent a *value* that sustains our "national predicament." The individual success stories that are promoted on the evening news, in best-selling memoirs, podcasts, and in sports and politics, reinforce this attention to the individual, leaving systems unexamined.

In the United States, this means that despite American values rooted in ideologies of progress and development, American master narratives are stunningly still. And this perspective on culture that centers structures and systems (e.g., laws, school policies) makes vivid the ways that power hierarchies are maintained by our values, as instantiated in our activities and practices.

Before closing this section, I do acknowledge that just as many of our activities work to sustain the status quo, we cannot overlook the activities of protest and resistance, which *have* resulted in powerful change (e.g., voting rights, though I fear where that will be as this book goes to print). I am not ignoring the topic of resistance to master narratives, and I will come back to it (Chapter 7). But the point here is that *change is hard in part because powerful people and entities prevent it with the stories they tell.*

HOW DID WE GET HERE? SOME HISTORY ABOUT THE SELF AND IDENTITY

When I was a new assistant professor, in my first job at the University of Toronto, I was eagerly reading all manner of theoretical and philosophical work on the self and identity. I was building my knowledge base as an independent researcher, finally feeling my own wings. I remember it as an exciting, if stressful, period of exploration. It was in this heady period when I came across a citation for a paper by Philip Cushman written 15 years prior called *Why the Self Is Empty: Toward a Historically Situated Psychology* (1990; see also Cushman, 1996). Cushman made the basic argument that our conceptions of self are intricately, intimately tied to our sociohistorical context. Most relevant to the current argument, he argued that post–World War II conceptions of self are rooted in the need to consume and acquire in order to be whole. We can fill the empty self by acquiring and consuming cars, televisions, and lifestyles made vivid and seductive by celebrities. And we can also fill those selves up through therapy and efforts toward self-improvement. A self that is defined by the need to acquire, a self that is empty, is a concept of self that serves the industries of both advertising and psychotherapy particularly well. Meaning that the industry—yes, industry—of psychology had helped to create the ills it sought to heal.

Cushman's ideas struck a chord. I actually have a memory of where I was sitting when I read that paper: I was on my tiny deck, crowded with pots of tomato plants and flowers, off my narrow apartment in Little Portugal in west Toronto—feeling a sense of unease as I absorbed the ideas. But I think at the time I was too green and too junior to get too deep into Cushman's argument because it would challenge so much of what I did, and of what I wanted to do. I was protective of my newly developing territory and passions. I wasn't ready to think about it in depth because of the insecurity it would engender, how it would *challenge the status quo* of how to do my work, with which I was quickly becoming comfortable. I understood *then* that his argument was that psychology is an industry, part of a consumerist ideology. What I understand *now* is that I am (we are) complicit in perpetuating ideologies that may be harmful and that may be based on less sound science than we would like to think. The insecurity I wished to avoid then has resurfaced now.

Cushman and the Empty Self

Cushman's argument that the United States has developed a culture of materialism and consumption that resulted in—which in fact required—"empty selves" that needed to be filled implicates not only the industry of advertising and celebrity culture but also the industries of self-improvement and personal growth, which are often sought through therapy. In a nutshell, the promise of personal growth and change is a cultural story that is told and sold.

Cushman traces conceptions of self through various philosophical and intellectual eras, from the increasingly individualistic notion of self elaborated by Enlightenment thinkers, to the sexually restricted self of the Victorian era, a history of thought that leads up to the current emphasis on "rational self-domination" (Cushman, 1996, p. 33). Such an ideology defines the self as conquerable, controllable, and ... changeable.

> the individual self came to be seen as the ultimate locus of salvation: the self was ever evolving, constantly changing, on a never-ending search for self-actualization and "growth." ... Personal fulfillment is seen as residing primarily within the individual, who is supposed to be self-sufficient and self-satisfied. For this self there are supposed to be no limits to achievement and enjoyment. (Cushman, 1996, p. 77)

This ideology is obviously seen in contemporary consumerism and messaging about the possibility of growth. But to me the darker part is that the ideology *promises change*. If we keep working and striving, we *will* be better. But the problem is that if there are no limits, then we are never done; we are always striving. And the message feeds an industry, with powerful interests that want the industry to thrive. Their bottom line, their economic livelihood, depends on your continued striving toward an undefined end—pretty clever economic strategy. What I take from Cushman is that the idea that you can change your story is not necessarily a psychological truth; it is a manufactured message.

So what purpose does the message serve?

> By psychologizing political problems, by interiorizing human beings, by valorizing an isolated individualism, by privileging cognitive processes above the material conditions of everyday life, by covertly providing a compensatory solution for a political problem instead of encouraging patients to explore the socio-political arrangements that caused the problem, current forms of psychotherapy also run the risk of contributing to the status quo in ways they would never consciously consent to. (Cushman, 1996, p. 130)

When we place the blame for poverty on individuals, we do not need to think about the systems and structures that create and sustain poverty.

When we see gender-based or race-based violence as the result of bad seeds, we are recused from thinking about how to change the systems of patriarchy and white supremacy; we are allowed to ignore the very soil from which such violence grows. When we vote to build a bigger jail rather than more housing, or don't talk about race with our (white) children because it is "too political" or they are "too young," we are denying the role of systems in our lives and in our identities. We are (likely unconsciously) believing in a story that makes us feel superior, and that lets us off the hook (Spencer, 2017).

So the idea that you can change your story is embedded in a cultural-historical context. It is an ideology created to sustain current systems and structures. And it is an ideology that prevents cultural and structural change that would actually improve the lives of individuals.

> One's allegiance is to oneself in the striving after individual health and revitalization. A liberation is promised, but it is entirely isolated, apolitical, individual liberation, which at bottom, of course, is no liberation at all. (Cushman, 1996, p. 69)

Cushman's work focused primarily on psychotherapy, though I think the ideas translate more broadly, such as to the industry of academic psychology and its messages about the self and the potential for growth. In particular, I think that the messages we sell work to sustain not only this consumerist ideology but also the academic systems needed by scholars and their respective institutions (e.g., the industry of journal publishing, tenure, grant funding, etc.).

But let me be clear: I do not necessarily think the majority of us in academia are intentionally building and sustaining this inequitable system. One of the premises of the master narrative framework is that such narratives are so pervasive as to be unconsciously internalized. In fact, that helps us to maintain our perception of agency—we think we are in control because we do not see the constraints on us. Like the body gets hijacked by a virus, we get hijacked by master narratives, passing them on with every lecture, every article, every trade book, and every Ted Talk.

But we are not helpless organisms. We can see the virus if we put our mind to it. Because time really is up—it's time to see how we are unwittingly adding to the spread of disease. Just as we have seen major shifts in our empirical practices with the advent of the replication crisis and the open science movement (e.g., Munafò et al., 2017; Spellman, 2015; Syed, 2019), a shift in how we approach the study of change is possible. And we might want to start by more closely examining our data to see that the story we have been selling about change is not based on the soundest empirical work.

Contemporary Examples: Posttraumatic Growth

Posttraumatic growth has been a hot topic in psychology. The idea is that a person experiences a horrible trauma—accident, illness, death of a loved one, and so on—and then that person changes in some way for the better. One of the first papers on the topic (Tedeschi & Calhoun, 1996) had a subtitle of "The Positive Legacies of Trauma." This concept has inspired hundreds of empirical papers and studies, most of which used one measure: a self-report survey about whether people *feel* they have grown after trauma (Tedeschi & Calhoun, 1996). Prompts asking people to evaluate themselves after the traumatic experience include the following:

I have more compassion for others.
I have a greater feeling of self-reliance.
I have a better understanding of spiritual matters.
I am more likely to try to change things that need changing.
I discovered that I'm stronger than I thought I was.

What researchers find is that people who agree with items like these also say they are happier and less depressed, for example (see Jayawickreme & Blackie, 2014, for a review). Such findings led researchers to the conclusion that posttraumatic growth can be observed as "positive psychological change experienced *as a result of* the struggle with highly challenging life circumstances" (Tedeschi & Calhoun, 2004, p. 1; emphasis in italics). But recently researchers have called such measurement into question

(Jayawickreme & Blackie, 2014; see also McLean, Fish, Rogers, & Syed, 2023), and for good reason: It does not measure actual change.

I was part of a group of researchers trying to study posttraumatic growth *prospectively*, and more objectively. We took measurements of aspects of people's personalities that we hypothesized, according to the theory, might possibly change after experiencing trauma or adversity, like compassion and life satisfaction. We took these measures before people experienced a challenging event and then looked to see if these things changed after the event. We were all interested in what predicted change, or growth. In the case of the team of which I was a part, we thought that the way someone narrated the story of adversity would predict if and how they grew post-adversity (Blackie & McLean, 2022). I sat in a room of about 10 research teams as each one got up to present their findings, showing that they couldn't even get at what might predict change because one of the major findings across studies was *how little people actually changed* (e.g., Blackie & McLean, 2022; Chopik et al., 2021; see also Lamade, Jayawickreme, Blackie, & McGrath, 2020). People might *think* they have changed from how they were before the event, but their actual scores pre- to post-event don't budge much.

Thinking you have changed is not for nothing. But why is thinking one has changed associated with such good things? One hypothesis is that the measure is asking if people buy into the master narrative, the cultural ideology, of personal growth. Do they buy the idea that we can grow from trauma? And if they do, they are fitting a cultural expectation, which makes them happier, or at least they report greater happiness. So the thing that makes you happy is not growth, but doing what is expected in the face of trauma: telling a good story about it.

This story can be defined as a *redemptive master narrative*, which is argued to play a particularly powerful role in adult development (e.g., McAdams, 2006). As people narrate challenges in their lives, those who see those challenges in a redemptive light—such as experiencing growth, emancipation, or enlightenment—are more generative and have greater psychological health than those who do not (e.g., McAdams & Guo, 2015). McAdams has also shown that this narrative is foundational in our culture. He traces the narrative through American history, religious texts, literature, and modern media, showing how much it shapes our past and our current culture. Its longevity, familiarity, and utility for making sense of trauma and adversity mean it is a narrative that people want to hear.

My colleagues and I have seen evidence of this cultural press for redemption, such that it is not only that this *story* is preferred by audiences but also that story*tellers* who use it are preferred (McLean, Delker, Dunlop, Salton, & Syed, 2020). That is, people who redeem their traumas are *liked more, thought to have better personalities, and to be more psychologically mature* than those who do not redeem their traumas. What does this mean for those who can't see silver linings? They will be liked less. Their stories will be liked less. They will be less likely to be *heard*.

Consider a story of a girl named Dasani, profiled in the *New York Times* (Elliot, 2021), who was born into a system of obstacles. Her grandfather fought in World War II with the Buffalo Soldiers, a segregated, all-Black regiment. He returned home with a triple bronze service star. Despite his training as a mechanic in the army, he was able to find only piecemeal low-wage jobs. He was unable to get a mortgage or to access GI benefits, finding his family a home in subsidized housing, which would eventually be known as "the projects." By the time Dasani was born, her family was experiencing homelessness and cycles of addiction. Despite these challenges, her mother fights to keep her close-knit family together. But the system is overwhelming at multiple turns. Obtaining shelter, food, and a reasonable commute to school are challenges. Finding affordable day care so that the adults can work is near impossible. And the list goes on.

But Dasani is smart, savvy, and motivated. She sees education as a way to lift herself and her family out of poverty, and she is saturated in the American narrative that this is the way out (hard work assuredly leads to success). At 13, she is accepted into a private school supposedly designed for kids like her, where she is provided shelter, food, clothes, routine, and of course, education. But she is forced into a new culture, housed with a white family, with a new language, what Dasani calls "talking white." Dasani laments, "If I talk the way I naturally talk—to them—like, something's wrong with me."

And she is separated from her family, who continue to struggle, leaving her with intense guilt and sadness at not being able to help them. Eventually the stress of assimilation and being apart from the people she loves the most is too much. The experiment doesn't work.

> For Dasani, succeeding at [school] would have required a different kind of death. It would have meant losing—even killing off—a basic part of herself. "It was like they wanted you to be someone that you wasn't," she says.

Despite Dasani's many exceptional personal characteristics, she is not the exception; she is the rule. And hers is not a redemption story. It doesn't fit the narrative that hard work pays off, that change is possible. It is not consistent with the cultural ideology that upholds systems of power. It is a story that provides a larger picture, not just of how Dasani gets up when she is knocked down, but about what keeps knocking her down. It is about the inability to get government support for day care without a paystub, and the inability to get a job to get the paystub without day care, the perpetuation of intergenerational trauma made possible by inequitable access to physical and mental health care, the lack of accumulation of intergenerational wealth created by laws that denied access to home ownership for Black veterans, and the lack of adequate schooling and housing in one of the richest nations in the world.

Even though this story was given a cover of the Sunday *New York Times* magazine, I suspect that it is one that many may easily forget. At one point, Dasani told the reporter, "I'm visible . . . But society doesn't see me."

So our press for and love of redemption is laden with consequences. It's upsetting to consider, and it lands like a discordant note, but your redemptive story comes at a cost to others. This love of redemption, even the redemptive stories from our own lives, is part of the system that uplifts stories of the almighty power of the individual.

I am not suggesting that the answer is to stop telling redemptive stories. The answer is to begin to realize that there is a "danger of the single story," as argued by writer Chimamanda Ngozi Adichie (2009). When we focus too much on one narrative, we exclude others.

THE COMPLICITY OF ACADEME IN THE PERPETUATION OF MASTER NARRATIVES

I worry that the emphasis we, academic psychologists, put on concepts such as redemption and posttraumatic growth, along with the agency that we think people have to create these kinds of stories, makes us complicit in a cultural press toward valuing particular kinds of stories and particular kinds of people, a "scientific polyannaism" (Yakushko, 2019; see also Ryff, 2022). We are complicit in pushing an ideology that leaves some people out in the cold and a story that allows us to ignore the system. Further, we play a part in perpetuating this idea that people can and do grow after trauma without always having very good data (see more on this in Chapter 4).

How exactly are we complicit? For one thing, we are biased in what we choose to study, who we study, and how we study it. Here is one example from my own research (there are many). When I first started studying stories and identity, I was into the idea of autobiographical reasoning (I still am) (e.g., Habermas & Bluck, 2000). I was reading hundreds of narratives of self-defining memories—vivid, emotional, important memories that explain who you are (e.g., Singer, Blagov, Berry, & Oost, 2013). I was capturing the degree to which people reported that they had learned something about themselves from the event they reported—did they gain any lessons or insights in reflecting on their story? I remember in one of the first manuscripts I submitted a reviewer asked about the valence of these meanings—were they positive or negative? I had never even thought about that. And it turned out that the great majority were positive—so many that it wasn't worth trying to capture valence because there was not enough variability to figure out why people might have positive or negative meanings. So what is the problem here? First, I hadn't thought about it seriously. Perhaps this was because my sample was pretty narrow—relatively privileged and mostly white college students, which may have been why the meanings were so positive (see subsequent work that challenges the positive meaning idea with different samples: e.g., McLean, Wood, & Breen, 2013; Sales, Merrill, & Fivush, 2013). I also didn't think about creating an assessment that would allow for various kinds of meaning. Not that I excluded negative meaning from my assessment, but I didn't consider whether or not my assessment *might* have precluded such meanings. Finally, I may have been drawn to the positive meanings precisely because I am a participant in the culture in which I work. I may have attended to these meanings and prioritized them in my analysis because they resonated with me, because I liked them. In short, I just didn't think about it in any careful way in terms of my scientific assessments and design, or in terms of my own reflexivity about my own biases. And, of course, all of this matters.

And we are complicit not only in how we conduct our research but also in how we communicate what we study. We are authorities with lots of power to shape narratives. I teach students, give lectures at other universities and talks at conferences, present at PTA meetings and local nonprofits, give interviews for media outlets, and of course publish in academic journals. We need to communicate our science, for sure. But before we get out there, talking about how great redemptive stories are and how much personal growth is possible after trauma, we need to be sure we have sound data. And we need to be sure we have adequately examined the broader contexts in which individuals function. I can't really say it better than Cushman did:

> If psychology is one of the guilds most responsible for determining the proper way of being human, then psychology wields a significant amount of power, especially in our current era, in which the moral authority of most religious and philosophical traditions has been called into question. By unknowingly propping up the hegemony of individualism through laboratory findings, psychology is preventing individuals from having the ability to see into how political structures impact the individual and how much these structures

are responsible for the suffering of the victims and the crimes of the perpetrators. (Cushman, 1996, p. 336)

Finally, we are complicit in not acknowledging our own biases as cultural beings in the culture we are studying. We are in the water in which we swim. When we tell a scientific story that doesn't meet cultural expectations, it is less likely to find approval, it is less likely to be heard. And, like everyone else, we want approval, and we want to be heard. Until we recognize that we are humans with values and motives, and understand how those values and motives impact what we study, we are in trouble (McLean & Syed, 2021).

I want to be clear that I include myself in these critiques. I have done the exact kinds of studies I am calling out. I have talked about the power of redemption, the beauty of it. I have seen it in my data! The story of triumph over tragedy *is* beautiful when it rings true. But, increasingly, I am starting to see that my focus, our focus, is missing something that we can no longer ignore. I hope we can take a step back to see if there is another path forward, or to see a larger landscape of stories (Pasupathi, 2021). And there *are* people doing this work. I will review the inspirational work of some of my colleagues who have been charting this larger landscape. But it will take a lot more people listening to these experts and changing how they do their work.

A big part of my motivation for writing this book is to make vivid the cultural press for these stories of personal growth and change, stories that are assumed to be under the control of the individual, and to articulate how constraining and harmful that cultural press may be. But a bigger motivation is to highlight the role that (most) psychologists have in perpetuating an ideology of growth and change that may be promising more than can be delivered, and that may be silencing stories and identities that do exist in our midst. As Dasani said, "I'm visible ... But society doesn't see me." We might learn something new if we looked. And listened.

# Theoretical Foundations

Identities, Stories, and Change

Now that the cultural-historical context in which individuals develop has been given its proper weight, we can begin to focus on those individuals and how they are intertwined with that larger context. As we move into this discussion of the potential for identity change, the first question I should answer is: *What do I mean by identity?*

I define identity broadly as knowing who you are, how you came to be this person, and what your purpose is. More specifically, it is defined by the development of an understanding of how you have existed across time: how you have developed across developmental stages, transitions, and various life experiences. It is understanding yourself as multifaceted—as a scholar, a parent, and a nonbinary white person, for example—and how those facets fit together. It is also understanding yourself as a member of a group: how you fit into the norms and expectations of your cultural community. Each of these types of understanding represents a particular type of identity *integration* (Syed & McLean, 2016): integration across *time*, integration across *context*, and integration with a *cultural group*. I'll detail each type of integration in what follows.

But it is important to note that although I have spent a good deal of time throughout my career examining processes of identity development that occur early in the lifespan, that is not my focus here. Here I am interested in later stages of development when people already have at least some integration or commitment to a particular identity. Because change does not come in the *formation* of identity, but in shifting from that which exists to something different.

INTEGRATION THROUGH TIME

Erik Erikson's (e.g., 1950, 1968) development of the concept of identity integration was in part inspired by his work with what he called shell-shocked veterans of World War II. He observed in these veterans a fragmentation of identity, or a lack of "sameness and continuity" (Friedman, 1999), such that the veterans' lives lacked coherence. They were unable to integrate the experience of themselves before, during, and after the war. This disjuncture across time created a crisis of self.

Temporal discontinuity was something Erikson also observed in himself upon the revelation of a troubling family secret. When he discovered that the man he thought was his father was not, it was an unmooring experience, creating a rift in his story about himself (Freidman, 1999). Erikson also wrote about what he learned from his work with the Yurok and Sioux nations,[1] how the colonizing violence, efforts to annihilate a people, and systemic denial of culture and practices created an intergenerational void that was (and is) experienced as a discontinuity of identity through time (Chandler, Lalonde, Sokol, & Hallett, 2003; Fish, Counts, Ruzzicone, Ogbeide, & Syed, 2023; Fish & Syed, 2018; Syed & Fish, 2018). Across all these kinds of experience—combat, family secrets, historical trauma, and genocide—we see how individuals face relational and contextual obstacles that undermine the experience of *persisting* through time.

---

1. See Syed and Fish (2018) for a discussion of the limitations and inaccuracies in the use of tribal names in Erikson's writings.

Being able to feel a sense of integration across time—that there is some sameness or continuity between the self that exists now and that self of 5 years ago, 10 years ago, and so on—offers two unique advantages for human functioning. First, it makes us responsible for our behaviors. If we can disregard past selves as not relevant to current selves, we can do whatever we want without consequence: "Well, that wasn't me." Temporal persistence allows for a moral responsibility to ourselves and to others (Chandler et al., 2003; Pasupathi, Mansour, & Brubaker, 2007). Second, seeing the self as persistent through time allows us to envision and channel the self into the future: "I've always been someone who makes it through hard times, and so I will in the future." Such a through line is a buffer for some of the most serious threats to the self, such as suicide (Chandler et al., 2003).

Finally, it is important to note that continuity does not mean *exactly the same*. Continuity means that we see something that links us through time, a through line. For example, in the following fictionalized account of autobiography, Tim O'Brien, himself a veteran of the Vietnam War, articulates this continuity and persistence:

> I'm forty-three years old . . . and yet when I look at photographs of myself as I was in 1956, I realize that in the important ways I haven't changed at all. I was Timmy then; now I'm Tim. But the essence remains the same. I'm not fooled by the baggy pants or the crew cut or the happy smile—I know my own eyes—and there is no doubt that the Timmy smiling at the camera is the Tim I am now. Inside the body, or beyond the body, there is something absolute and unchanging. The human life is all one thing, like a blade tracing loops on the ice: a little kid, a twenty-three-year-old infantry sergeant, a middle-aged writer knowing guilt and sorrow. (O'Brien, 1990, p. 236)

Unlike the veterans Erikson studied, O'Brien portrays a self that engaged in the horrors of war (see this story and others in *The Things They Carried*) and yet is still able to find a sense of temporal integration that keeps him tethered to the world.

INTEGRATION ACROSS CONTEXTS

Beyond time, we also need to understand ourselves as having some continuity across different contexts. We exist in different *identity domains*, such as how we define ourselves in relationships (e.g., as romantic partners, parents, friends), our ideologies (e.g., religious or political beliefs), or our social identities (e.g., gender, ethnicity). Some aspects of these contexts are relevant to most people, such as occupational identity, and some are highly individualized, such as being a San Franciscan born in 1976 in the Haight Ashbury, for example. It is the domains or contexts that are important to the person that are likely to be central to identity. For example, being agnostic is not highly important to me, but my identity as a Californian, as a San Franciscan, is.

And, critically, it is not only the individual who "decides" what is important; the context has a say as well. I could argue that my white racial identity is not especially salient or important to me in the culture of white supremacy in which I live. But this is less likely to be the case for those who are Black, Brown, and Indigenous. Racial and ethnic identities are not made more or less salient or important only by virtue of *personal* meaning but also by virtue of *cultural* meaning (see Erikson, 1968; Rogers, 2018; Tatum, 2000).

In terms of integration, or lack of it, in Erikson's work with the veterans he saw that they not only had trouble seeing a sense of continuity through time (before, during, and after the war), they also had trouble reconciling parts of themselves when they returned, such as the selves they were with their fellow veterans at the VFW post versus in their homes or at work. The fragmentation here comes from the disjuncture between their selves across different contexts.

When people find this disjuncture distressing, figuring out how to put the pieces together brings a satisfying feeling of coherent integration. In a contemporary example, I conducted a longitudinal study with Jennifer Pals Lilgendahl, the Identity Pathways Project, in which we examined how college students understood themselves across time and in various contexts. One of our participants wrote about how she found an integration between her academic pursuits and other interests (see McLean, Koepf, & Lilgendahl, 2022):

> I realized that I was not passionate about Pharmacy at all, and that I was only taking that path because it was what was expected of me and was convenient. I turned towards Geology because I realized that through all of my hobbies/interests, Geology and how the earth works is the one that has stuck with me since I was a child. I love being outside and understanding the Earth, and I realized that if I wanted to get deeper into it—now was the time to take that life path.

This kind of integration between her interests and her academic major creates a sense of unity and purpose. Incidentally, she also gets a little temporal integration in as well, by seeing her interest in the Earth as one that has persisted through time, which helps her to chart a path forward.

INTEGRATION AND CULTURAL BELONGING

Beyond the specific contexts of a workplace or classroom, for example, there is also a need to fit with the larger culture. Cultural messages, ideologies, and master and alternative narratives give us lots of information about where we belong. The master narrative framework discussed in Chapter 2 is explicit about the ways that cultural stories favor some people, groups, and stories over others. Some people are easily able to fit in with mainstream expectations and to benefit from that alignment in terms of status, power, and psychological comfort. For those whose identities are misrepresented, or who are not represented, within the larger culture, a sense of discontinuity can be marked.

In another example from the Identity Pathways Project, we can see how the challenge of cultural belonging is experienced during a major developmental experience—the transition to college—as reported by a student in her third year at university (see Patterson et al., 2022):

> I didn't realize how hard my transition into college was until the past year or so. It hasn't been until I realized and accepted that I wasn't like my peers who had grown up in the [S]tates.... While I was transitioning to the [S]tates I wasn't actively thinking that it was a challenge, but looking back on it I have realized that when I was struggling or having a hard time the main cause could be linked to some sort of culture shock and a feeling of being out of place. It took me a while to realize this and I think as a freshman I was trying to push away my Arab-ness in order to fit in and it led me to this sort of identity crisis and I had no idea what I wanted or if I wanted to stay ... I remember the like anxiety I would have going to the niche stores downtown or something just because I didn't really know the culture and I never connected the dots before.

The distress of cultural disconnect that this student articulates is seen within particular subcultures and groups who do not align with master narratives. Nic Weststrate and I (e.g., Weststrate, 2021; Weststrate & McLean, 2010, 2022) have been working for years on understanding the consequences of the societal marginalization of minoritized sexual identities. One man in a study of ours who identified as gay and who came of age in the 1960s reported:

> In Grade 9 I consented to a clandestine rendezvous with a male classmate at the supper hour back at the school locker room. It was one of the few times in my teens when I had sexual contact. The feel of another male body was exciting. However, my cultured guilt took over for several years before I was truly able to sort my true feelings out. Back then, there were very few people to talk to in a small town.

For this man, not fitting in with cultural expectations about sexuality leads to silencing and hiding parts of the self that are deeply important and central to who he is (Fivush, 2004, 2010). Moreover, this example shows how trying to understand oneself is deeply constrained by access to developmental resources, such as contact with others who have similar identities and cultural stories to share that help to build a sense of connection (Turner, Weststrate, & McLean, 2023; Weststrate & McLean, 2022; Weststrate, Turner, & McLean, 2023).

Tragically, not only does this individual struggle to find integration, but the rest of us also lose out by not hearing his stories. We lose the chance to see something different from our own experiences, to learn something. Or to see similarity where we thought there would be none, perhaps to develop empathy. We may even lose the chance to embrace ourselves more fully—the more variety we accept, even celebrate, in others, perhaps the more we can be who we are. And, of course, by not hearing these stories we lose the chance to understand what needs changing to better our collective well-being. The perpetuation of cultural silence about particular identities has consequences for both the individual and society (see also Fivush, 2004).

PERSONAL AND COLLECTIVE RESPONSIBILITY FOR THE WORK OF IDENTITY INTEGRATION

Understanding one's identity through time, across contexts, and in reference to cultural expectations is a complicated process. Each of these forms of integration does not come easily; it takes time and effort to move through the possibilities, uncertainties, and roadblocks to find what makes us feel whole. And, perhaps something of a paradox, once we have done this hard developmental work, once we experience this sense of integration, we get attached to this identity we have constructed and it becomes harder to change. When we work for something, we are more committed to it, more invested in it. And so it is that much harder to let go. When the young woman works through a series of challenges in deciding to shift her major from Pharmacy to Geology, she feels a sense of wholeness in that decision. She starts to define herself in this domain, perhaps finding a community of people who share her interests, beginning to imagine her future career. However, each of these components of identity commitment means that it will be harder to let it go, to change that part of her identity if a desire for change arises down the line. Of course, she may not *need* to let it go. She may have found her path and her place, and then experience the satisfaction and joy that come with such integration of self. But once we choose one path, once we travel down it, it is important to acknowledge that it becomes harder and harder to change directions.

But it is not just one's *own* investment in an identity that makes it hard to change. It is also the case that the investment *others* have in our identities makes it hard for *them* to let parts of our identities go (McLean, 2015). For the Geology major, her friends, parents, mentors, and teachers may share the investment that she develops, and the expectations for her future. You have a collective of people invested in something as it is. And that same collective of people may be puzzled if she later expresses herself differently. In short, the expectations of the collective can be supportive and validating—until one feels the need to shift.

The Additional Challenges of Identity Work for Those on the Margins

When one is not sure of one's path, the resulting dissonance demands attention. This dissonance has typically been described as most prominently felt in late adolescence and emerging adulthood (Erikson, 1968), especially in industrialized and Western contexts. However, there are emerging pieces of evidence suggesting that the age-based developmental timeline may not be accurate for those who are developing identities on the margins. For example, in the United States, children of color are engaged in understanding their racial and ethnic identities earlier than white children (e.g., Rogers & Way, 2018; Rogers, Rosario, Padilla, & Foo, 2021; Umaña-Taylor et al., 2014), and LGBTQ+ youth may engage in some aspects of their identity work later than their straight and cisgendered counterparts (Turner et al., 2023). These examples show that when scholars don't think about the hegemonic systems that drive our work, we neglect to consider how what we view as "normative" is so often defined by those with structurally privileged identities (see also McLean & Riggs, 2022; Rogers et al., 2023).

For the developing human being, a societal and cultural *devaluing or denial* of central parts of oneself also results in an intensified labor of identity integration. For example, my colleagues and I have found that those with structurally marginalized identities—in one study defined as identifying as LGBTQ+, a woman, non-white, or of lower socioeconomic status—reported greater effort toward understanding their identities (McLean et al., 2018). This is consistent with the substantial literature that shows youth of color report more exploration of and attributed more importance to their racial and ethnic identities than white youth (e.g., Umaña-Taylor et al., 2014). In short, being in a marginalized position is associated with more intensive identity work than those who exist in locations of privilege where one's identity is not questioned, distorted, or denied.

There is also a substantial literature revealing the broader challenges for those who are not in positions of power to navigate their different identities within mainstream culture. For example, students of color at predominantly white institutions (e.g., Harper, 2015; Morrison, 2010; Syed, Azmitia, & Cooper, 2011), first-generation college students (e.g., Langhout, Drake, & Rosselli, 2009), and women in certain scientific and tech-focused workplaces (e.g., Trinkenreich, Britto, Gerosa, & Steinmacher, 2022) are more likely to experience a sense of disconnection between the selves they experience at school or work, and selves expressed in their families or home communities. White and male-dominated contexts demand a certain kind of presentation of self (at least to succeed at mainstream expectations) that marginalizes those who are not white and male. Further, for those who do not fit with the master narratives, the success of those who do looks easy, adding an additional burden to those already facing obstacles. These challenges and feelings of persistent disconnection are associated with lower rates of perseverance in education, disrupted career trajectories, and general stress and dissatisfaction.

The Need for Systemic Change So That All Identities Can Flourish

But if the work of identity integration is not fruitful, the conclusion should not be that the individual has not worked hard enough. A structural perspective on identity development illuminates how systemic inequities can restrict access to experiencing integrated and valued selves (Syed & McLean, 2022a). From this perspective it becomes clear that "the work" should not be entirely on the shoulders of the individual. When a group is *systematically and structurally* marginalized by mainstream society, addressing cultural exclusion so that individuals *can* experience a sense of integration, so that they *want* to be included in such a culture, is the responsibility of the collective, and it involves systemic change.

The experience of Native Americans provides a compelling example of the need for systemic change to support identity integration. Jill Fish (Fish & Syed, 2018) situates such an argument in the context of education, which has perpetuated harm through forced assimilation in residential schools, blocking access to educational pathways, the systematic denial of the histories and experiences of Native American students for generations, and the celebration of colonization. A sense of disconnection is practically guaranteed, and the responsibility to address that disconnection lies with the institution, in this case institutions of higher learning. Fish writes:

> it is crucial that higher education professionals dismantle features of institutions that dishonor the collective memory of Native American students. For example, the Biology department at Amherst College once displayed posters of Jeffrey Amherst, pioneer in biological warfare, presenting Native Americans with blankets—a reference to Amherst's use of smallpox to gain military advantage against Native Americans in Pontiac's war (Landry, 2012). Similarly correcting inaccurate histories (e.g., a college or university recognizing Columbus Day), negative stereotypes (e.g., Native American mascots), and the degradation of Native American culture (e.g., Cal Poly's Phi Sigma

Kappa's "Colonial Bros and Nava-Hos" party; Hickey, 2013) will help dismantle institutional racism. (Fish & Syed, 2018, p. 392)

Thus, to sum up: The project of identity development centers on developing a sense of integration across time, context, and within one's culture. The task of integration takes both individual work and collective work. Once people experience a sense of integration, change becomes more challenging because there is a certain level of commitment to one's identity. And the perpetuation of an inequitable system means that some are tasked with a greater burden to develop an identity that provides that sense of integration. Which means that we need systemic change to facilitate an integration that betters individual lives and the larger society (see Rogers & Way, 2021).

I keep referring to the "work" of integration. So what does that work look like? The foundation of my research is that a major mechanism, or activity, of integration is storytelling. Narrative is a way to develop a sense of identity integration. And narrative exists at both individual and cultural levels.

STORYING IDENTITY

There are a lot of approaches to measuring and conceptualizing identity. Many assessments of identity development focus on the measurement of the *degree* of exploring one does, or the *degree* of commitment one experiences (e.g., Luyckx, Goossens, & Soenens, 2006; Marcia, 1966). But such measures are often devoid of context or content, such as *what* one is exploring, or *where and when* someone is exploring (see also Syed, 2022, for a review of the necessity of attending to time and context in measurement). And few assessments focus on actual activities or practices. I like to situate my examination of identity development on stories, because storytelling is one of the oldest, and most common, activities in which humans engage. We tell stories *all the time* (see McLean, Pasupathi, & Pals, 2007, for a review). Storytelling serves multiple purposes from communicating values and history, providing entertainment, helping to develop intimate bonds, and, of course, developing identities (e.g., Bluck & Alea, 2009). Through storytelling we can construct a sense of self through time, across contexts, and within a cultural group. Narration is a way both to understand and to communicate who we are (Cohler, 1982; Fivush, 2019; McAdams, 1988, 1993; Sarbin, 1986).

What Do I Mean by Story?

Your story is not your circumstances. It's not the money in your bank account, the kind of car you drive, or where you live. It's not how much you drink at night or how often you go to the gym. Nor is it whether you are single, married, divorced, or widowed. Of course, circumstances are important—whether you are rich or poor, get sober or keep drinking, get divorced or stay married—these are deeply significant parts of a life. But I am focused not on the *facts* of the circumstances, but on the *meaning* that people make of these circumstances. How does a person tell the story of his divorce? How is it interpreted? How do others respond to it and shape that interpretation? And how does that interpretation of divorce connect to other events in a person's life, to create a narrative through line of self-understanding? Doing these three things—narrating past events, making meaning of them, and seeing the connections between them—is the main process by which people develop an integrated identity (e.g., Habermas & Bluck, 2000; McAdams, 1993, 2001; Syed & McLean, 2016).

The major premise of the study of narrative identity is that the subjective interpretation of past events is both an activity of development—this is how we actually *develop* an understanding of ourselves—and it is also a way to define ourselves to others once that self-knowledge is built. For example, as children and adolescents share past events with others, those conversations provide a mechanism for understanding what those events mean to them (Fivush, Haden, & Reese, 2006; McLean & Mansfield, 2011; Reese, Jack, & White, 2010). Over time, narrative activity broadens and deepens as adolescents not only narrate and interpret singular events but also become able to string them together to form a life story over time, a story that eventually becomes one's narrative identity (Habermas & de Silveira, 2008).

Storying ourselves is a mechanism for developing the kinds of integration I have detailed. And narration is a powerful way to understand and communicate selves because stories have explanatory power. Stories are ways of making arguments; they are good evidence. When the Geology student told her story about choosing a major, she explained how different parts of herself fit together, and how those interests show persistence through time. If this student simply said she chose Geology as a major with no explanation, with no connection to her life and experiences, it would fall pretty flat, as if the choice came out of thin air. To make that temporal and contextual integration vivid in a story is more convincing—both to her *and* to her audiences; it increases the level of commitment and certainty about who she is. But, on the flip side, that commitment and feeling of certainty make it that much harder to change the story.

Theoretical Perspective on Narration, the Role of Others, and the Possibility of Change

Change is a tricky concept. Sometimes it just means that we have moved a statistically significant notch on a scale assessment of some aspect of personality or self-understanding. Sometimes it is a preregistered measure of effect size on that scale. But I am not really interested in the relatively small movements on scales that we typically observe (see Chapter 4). I am more interested in the fundamental reorganization or reimagining of how we understand ourselves through time, across contexts, and in alignment or misalignment with the broader culture. I mean Big Change. Change that means we will interact with others in new ways, that our lives will be different, and change that will take a lot of work to create a story that serves us better than the old one.

In subsequent chapters I will detail the ways that we define and measure change for several aspects of personality, including narrative identity. But first it is necessary to lay out the different approaches to the scholarship on narrative identity, to see how these approaches have different expectations about *whether to expect change* in narrative identity.

I see the field of narrative identity as having at least three root systems. The first is in personality psychology, which focuses on individual differences in the ways that meaningful stories are narrated in terms of their implications for psychosocial development and functioning (e.g., Adler et al., 2016; McAdams & McLean, 2013; McLean et al., 2020). The second is in developmental psychology, where researchers have shown that a major mechanism of children's early self-concept development is the narration of the personal past in conversation with parents (e.g., Fivush, 2019; Nelson & Fivush, 2004). The third is the cultural perspective on master narratives that I have been discussing, and which grew from personality and developmental perspectives, bringing with it the emphasis on structure and power (McLean & Syed, 2015; Syed & McLean, 2021a; see also Hammack, 2008). Although each of these theories comes to the same conclusion—that storytelling is critical to understanding identity—the varying emphases in each of these root systems are truly distinct, particularly when it comes to the role of other people and how change is conceptualized.

Personality Approaches to Narrative Identity

Researchers who are more rooted in personality psychology have focused almost exclusively on how individuals narrate their past experiences solo, using written or interview assessments. These choices suggest that narrative identity is relatively accessible and relatively devoid of context. To be clear, I think that those of us working in this tradition do believe there is a context to narration, and many of us write about it and include it in our theorizing (e.g., Bauer, 2021; Hammack, 2008; McAdams & Pals, 2006; McLean et al., 2007; Pasupathi et al., 2007; Syed & McLean, 2021). But too often context is not factored into study design and assessment, which reveals priorities. And I see that the priority, in this field, is on the internalized story, rather than on the context. The second implication of these methodological choices is that the story that is told to the researcher is viewed to be relatively stable. It is a story carried around within the person that can be produced in a research context for an assessment of stable individual differences. Thus, it is not presumed to vary wildly or to change dramatically due to the context.

Indeed, from a personality perspective, narrative identity *has* to show some stability, as that is the definition of personality—individual differences in *characteristic* ways of being. Some of the foundational empirical work in the field of narrative identity was designed to show that there was stability in the ways that people narrate events over time, such as in the emotional tone or the complexity of stories (McAdams et al., 2006). That is, people who tell stories in a more negative way continue to do so over time. Many of us working in this tradition also choose to aggregate characteristics of narratives across multiple stories, which also assumes some consistency in how we narrate (e.g., Blagov & Singer, 2004; Mansfield, Pasupathi, & McLean, 2015; McAdams et al., 2004; McLean, Breen, & Fournier, 2010; but see Booker, Brakke, Sales, & Fivush, 2022; McLean, Pasupathi, Greenhoot, & Fivush, 2017; Pasupathi, Fivush, Greenhoot, & McLean, 2020). That said, in thinking about the various layers of personality, narrative *is* a more malleable aspect of ourselves than personality traits (McAdams & Pals, 2006). For example, we expect that as someone experiences particularly dramatic life events that there may be some kind of movement. Getting married, coming out of the closet, having a child, losing a parent—surely these types of events provide at least the opportunity to reevaluate oneself and one's story, and potentially to change parts of that story (see McLean, Köber, & Haraldsson, 2019; Chapter 5). But even with that, the emphasis in this field is still on relative stability and less empirical attention to context, compared to other fields.

Developmental Approaches to Narrative Identity

The developmentalists have primarily examined the development of narration in the social contexts of parent–child conversations about past events.

This methodological choice means that there is *always* a social interaction at the center of assessments (e.g., Nelson & Fivush, 2004). Interestingly, as children develop and move into adolescence and emerging adulthood, their ability to narrate the past improves, and they are presumed to need less structural support from others to construct stories. Consequently, most of our assessments (but not all—see, e.g., McLean & Mansfield, 2011; Pasupathi & Hoyt, 2009; Pasupathi & Rich, 2005) turn toward a more individual focus. We start interviewing people and asking for written assessments, adopting the personality approaches, assuming that narration has somehow turned inward.

However, it is now clear that others continue to be important in storying ourselves, not only as audiences and people who help us to construct our stories but also as people who tell stories *about* us. Others' stories define us just as much as our own stories (McLean, 2015; Fivush, 2019). Critically, as much as we are invested in our own stories, so too are others invested in our stories. In fact, much of our story once we reach adulthood has come from other people, with whom we may or may not agree. Our parents and families have a primary role in defining us in our early years. And even as we become more autonomous in interpreting the past, the weight of others and their stake in our identities is large (McLean, 2015). It's hard to resist the story told by the people we rely upon when we are developmentally vulnerable. All of this portends the challenge of change.

And couple this challenge with the growing realization across adolescence about the ways in which cultural stories may not serve us. As we move into the stage of life where we assume some autonomy in charting our life course, but with a story that has been so deeply coauthored, we may begin to bristle at the constraints we have experienced so far. We may notice some patterns that are not serving us, or experiences that we cannot navigate with our current story. And the need to change something emerges.

From a developmental perspective, there is plenty of room for change. At the most basic level, memory, in the form of narrative, is constructed in every context of recall and depends on our mood, why we're sharing the story, or what we've just been thinking about (e.g., Bartlett, 1932;

Fivush, 2011; Tversky & Marsh, 2000). We also change our evaluation of past events as, for example, the negative affect of difficult past events fades (e.g., Skowronski, Walker, Henderson, & Bond, 2014). And we shape the same story differently for distinct audiences (e.g., Hyman, 1994; Pasupathi, McLean, Weeks, & Hynes, 2019).[2] However, it is important to note that although, theoretically, there is room for change, long-term identity change has not been a focus of this work (see Chapter 5).

So personality perspectives prioritize stability, and developmental perspectives prioritize malleability. However, most working within these perspectives have not traditionally emphasized the role of structural components of society in identity development. And neither have most working in these domains traditionally considered the role of power and privilege in processes of identity development and change.

Master Narrative Approaches to Narrative Identity

As I articulated in Chapter 2, from the structural-psychological perspective that I take (Syed & McLean, 2022), master narratives dictate the kinds of selves we should be and stories we should tell. These expectations are communicated interpersonally, as well as through cultural mediums such as books, movies, and advertisements. When we see the insurance commercial showing the journey from a wedding day to a home purchase, to the birth of a child, to the graduation of that child, culminating with retirement and grandparenthood, many of us get teary. That's the story that we're supposed to want. That's the story we're supposed to have. It's a story that resonates with the cultural occupants of this society. But a master narrative approach also sees these stories reflected in structures, which facilitate and restrict access to certain lives and experiences. When we remember to see how the legal system has restricted marriage for some, how racism and income inequality deny access to home ownership

---

2. Notably, however, the great bulk of work in cognitive psychology has not examined the kind of self-defining stories that make up narrative identity.

for some, how supports necessary for childbearing and rearing—ranging from health care and day care to adoption and fertility treatments—shape life courses, we see how societal structures restrict access to these lives and stories. And that's not even touching whether one actually *wants* the life story depicted in the commercial. But the point is that structural constraints may make these experiences less possible and less desirable for some. Choices and desires do not only arise from the individual; they are also shaped by the structure of society.

In terms of whether to expect change in stories, the master narrative approach highlights how challenging such change is in two ways. On the cultural level, we have established how notoriously challenging it is to shift cultural stories as they are entrenched in foundational texts, concrete systems and structures, and through the generations of storytellers who serve to maintain the status quo. On the personal level, these cultural expectations create a strong scaffold to support the process of identity development. Those who get married, buy the house, and have the baby have a very clear template to follow. But the strength of that support means that changing one's story is quite difficult. Deviating from that script comes with sanctions, meaning there is less room for fluidity and shifting. There *may* be more room for change when one shifts *into* alignment with a master narrative, rather than deviating from it (see Chapter 6 for more discussion of this idea).

But, in general, when we consider systems, structures, and power, narrative change is pretty tough to come by.

WHY IS CHANGE HARD?

A primary function of narrative is to provide a structure for interpreting experience, a way to tell the story of what happens to us. For it to be a useful structure, there needs to be a predictability to how we narrate experiences in general (e.g., a beginning, a middle, and an end to the story in many cultures; Labov & Waletzky, 1967) and a predictability to how we narrate particular types of stories (e.g., the American propensity for redeeming adversity discussed in Chapter 2; McAdams, 2006). If the rules for how to tell stories are not relatively steadfast, we are adrift when we want to recall, share, respond to, and interpret past experiences. Therefore, one of the primary functions of narrative, one of the reasons it is so useful to us, is the rigidity of its format. This rigidity also makes it hard to change stories. In other words, the idea that stories can be changed at will has cultural currency, but it is not consistent with the actual function of narrative.

The Importance of Prediction and Control: Ontological Security

Changing a story that has been established and enforced is like learning to dribble a basketball with your nondominant hand. You have to silence old patterns that are comfortable and familiar, and that you are good at. It also means experiencing failure and uncertainty. Feeling uncertainty about who you are is unsettling, to say the least.

Our stories and identities are also, of course, very important to us. They represent our values and commitments, our place in our communities, our purpose in life (McAdams, 2001). To reevaluate our understanding of who we are brings into question whether and how we belong, clouds our futures, and threatens parts of us we may hold dear, parts that we may need to let go of, even to grieve, in restorying ourselves.

At base, all of these concerns arise from our human need for predictability and self-preservation. We are designed to be attuned to our environment so that we know what to expect and are ready to react. Over evolutionary time, however, it is not just that we are designed to orient toward prediction, the development of the prefrontal cortex means that we have developed empirical ways of thinking that make us *think* we can predict things. We expect the world to be orderly. When it isn't, we will go through all sorts of mental contortions to make it seem orderly once more.

For example, we will continue to believe unhealthy ideas about ourselves because those ideas are familiar—to the extent that, if we think poorly of ourselves, we are drawn to those who also devalue us because they confirm our self-views (Swann, 2012). We are also drawn to information that confirms our existing worldviews (e.g., Bessi et al., 2015; Del Vicario et al., 2016): We choose to watch MSNBC or Fox because the messages and arguments resonate with what we already believe. In fact, social media companies know this and design their algorithms so that we see posts that we are prone to "like" rather than expose us to posts that might make us uncomfortable or offer the opportunity to learn something (e.g., Cinelli et al., 2020). We use less analytical forms of reasoning to preserve belief systems that are important to us (e.g., McPhetres & Zuckerman, 2017); we don't want to think too hard about our most precious ideas as we may see the cracks in them. We uphold beliefs in the status quo to preserve certainty and security, even when the status quo does not serve us (e.g., Jost et al., 2017). So there is a lot of evidence that we will go to great lengths to protect our current views of ourselves to avoid uncertainty.

Although this need for predictability and certainty has been studied in many domains, Giddens (1991) argues that the need for order, or ontological security, is a phenomenon uniquely met by narrative because stories can provide a sense of predictability. We can make sense of things in ways that are comfortable or comforting and that make us feel as though we are in control. As Jefferson Singer (1997, p. 290) writes:

> rather than accept our complicated and ultimately unknowable relationship with the world, humans attempt to name the world, to become its author.

I think the field of narrative identity generally has had a much rosier view on stories, seeing them as opportunities for growth and development, a view I have shared and that I think still has validity. But the framing I am offering around prediction changes things a bit by emphasizing stories as serving basic needs for control. Using stories for prediction and control also allows individuals to tune out the larger systems, structures, and realities of the world in which we exist (Chapter 2). When we think we are in control of our own story, we assume others are as well. For some of us this is more problematic than for others, depending on where we are situated in the system.

Cultural Stories as Obstacles to Change

Some of these obstacles to personal identity change I have articulated impact the potential for cultural stories to change too. The need for predictability and the desire to maintain the status quo are also present at a structural level. Those in power, who benefit from policy and legislation, for example, would like to maintain such systems, and they use stories to do so. The power of stories becomes pretty tangible when you see how they are used to legislate, incarcerate, and educate.

There are myriad examples of how cultural stories are shaped to perpetuate the status quo. Jelani Cobb's analysis of the history of the Kerner Commission and protests about the continued stagnation on racial equity is one (Chapter 2). Another is well articulated by Bryan Stevenson of the Equal Justice Initiative, who is making a concerted effort to tell a different kind of story about race in America, articulating how cultural stories are tied to our current systems. In an interview in January 2020, Stevenson discussed the challenge of this change:

> Well, I mean, obviously, in the Deep South, there has been this whole effort to create a landscape that defends and romanticizes this period of enslavement and violence. When I moved to Montgomery, there were 59 markers and memorials in downtown Montgomery that talked unapologetically about the glory of the Confederacy, that era. Alabama even today still celebrates Jefferson Davis's birthday as a state holiday. Confederate Memorial Day in Alabama is a state holiday. We do not have Martin Luther King Day in Alabama. We have Martin Luther King/Robert E. Lee Day.

The master narrative about race is instantiated in the structures of our culture (e.g., holidays, school textbooks, current laws; see also Alexander, 2010), as well as in our personal stories.

In this interview, Stevenson goes on to say that for the Black students at Robert E. Lee High School in Montgomery, Alabama, for example, "you're just kind of required to accept this cultural environment that is hostile to the history that Black people have had to endure, that is indifferent to the violence and degradation that slavery represents." The internalization of this master narrative of race can result in the fragmented identities that manifest when personal experiences do not fit with these cultural stories. And the internalization that Stevenson speaks about means that the story of the status quo is maintained. Even if Black youth are exposed to alternative narratives in their families and communities about a more truthful past, along with stories of community strength, the task of integrating and negotiating these two types of stories is hard. For the Black youth there is more identity work to do. And there is no guarantee that the alternative narratives developed within Black families and communities will be heard at the mainstream level in a way that propels change. And this work of integration and negotiation is not a task that is pressing for those whose lives align with mainstream stories. For those white students who internalize mainstream cultural stories, their personal stories will uphold these cultural stories that perpetuate oppression, creating little motivation toward change because the cultural stories are "indifferent" to a violent past (and present).

In another domain, Jefferson Singer (1997) wrote a searing book about addiction and stories, *Message in a Bottle*, in which he detailed the ways in which cultural stories and systems restrict needed change for those on the margins. The book details heartbreaking life stories of men who are experiencing extreme, often lifetime, addiction. These men do not get better. They do not recover. There is little redemption. In exploring the lack of recovery, Singer points to a variety of reasons that these men *cannot change their identities* in ways that might free them from addiction. He details the inadequate cultural narratives about the reality of being Black, Brown, and impoverished men in America coupled with the relentless emphasis on the American Dream. He writes eloquently about the failed promises enshrined in the narrative expectations of Alcoholics Anonymous. These available narratives of grit and personal redemption through the hard work of recovery do not fit with the experiences of these men. These master narratives do not realistically account for the trauma of childhood abuse, of war, of poverty, racism, and homophobia, of absent parents. These men could not rewrite their way out of addiction and into the larger culture in part because the available story structures were deficient.

Most important, Singer writes that the fate of these men is not only a problem for them; their lack of recovery also poses problems for the larger community:

> another potential reason we fear the chronically addicted and maintain our disconnection from them is that they challenge us to consider the inadequacy of our stories—our representations—to account for the world we inhabit. The inexplicability of their addictive behavior and the ineffectiveness of our conventional stories to help them in their lives parallels the unknowability of the world that neither religion nor science has conquered. . . . Paradoxically . . . we may also find a bridge between our worlds. By accepting the *limits of our stories*, our ultimate failure to author the world, we are acknowledging our commonality with the man sleeping on the sidewalk. We are no longer separated by competing stories. . . . We become fellow characters in a common story, and our goal is no longer to replace one story with another, but to enter into a dialogue and exchange of shared experience. (p. 290, emphasis in italics)

Singer's clinical work, Stevenson's historical work, and the intentions behind the Kerner Commission point to the same issue: the need to revise our shared history to understand our selves and each other, and to understand how change might come about (see also Spencer, 2017, on shared vulnerability).

Embeddedness de-emphasizes the heroic aspect of our story-making, but in doing so allows us to become part of the larger supporting cast that shares a mutual responsibility to each other. Rather than seeing the project of life as focused on the fashioning of a tale, embeddedness encourages us to listen. The *problem of seeing identity as a story about how the individual creates meaning in the world is that this formulation loses sight of the individual's already existing place within the world. . . .* An awareness of embeddedness would lead to obligation. . . . If one's existence is embedded in a larger story, *the possibility of choosing to enter or exit that story does not exist.* (Singer, 1997, pp. 290, 292–293; emphasis in italics)

One of my colleagues, Nic Weststrate, calls stories "developmental resources" (Weststrate et al., 2023), much like having an attentive parent or access to healthy food and a good school. And he argues that those resources are not distributed equitably. The men with whom Singer worked and who were crushed by their addictions, the World War II veterans and Native Americans about whom Erikson wrote, the man who had the clandestine experience in the bathroom, the students at Robert E. Lee High School, and the many others who are placed on the margins by American society, are often denied access to mainstream cultural stories in which they see themselves represented truthfully and positively, the kinds of stories that are necessary to the work of identity development, and that lead to the experience of integration and coherence.

But I want to be clear that I am not intending to paint those on the margins as passive victims, waiting to receive better and healthier stories and resources. This raises a struggle and discomfort I have in the structure of this book. I could structure my argument so that the next point is: *although reducing the emphasis on individual characteristics like resilience and strength is important to draw attention to needed systemic and structural change, it is also important to recognize that there are alternative narratives of resilience in marginalized communities.* I could go on to discuss how these alternative narratives can provide a balm to the isolation and oppression of the experience of marginalization, a place to feel belonging and connection (Rogers & Way, 2021; Syed & McLean, 2022a), a place to see oneself represented in story, *as well as a place to cultivate resistance* (Rogers & Way, 2021; Chapter 7). I could foreground these alternative stories of resistance and the theories and approaches employed to examine the strength that can thrive in the face of oppression. But I am saving this discussion until Chapter 7. The reason I am doing that is I want to go heavy on the responsibility of the collective in changing systems, in the role of privileged stories and privileged people in maintaining the status quo. I want to make that argument unignorable and then move to a more complicated discussion of the agency of resistance among those who have been placed on the margins.

It is not because I think these alternative stories are less important. It is because I think these stories can be used, or misused, to further reify the power of the individual, to put the responsibility on the individual to resist, to take away from seeing the collective responsibility we share to resist and to change. Because the fact that some individuals have survived the crushing weight of master narratives and systemic oppression across generations, and even thrived, is not a testament to the American Dream. It is a warning for the need to broaden the scope of responsibility for needed change, so that individuals can develop their own stories under supportive cultural conditions.

The shift I am proposing is also not toward a complete lack of responsibility for the individual. I am suggesting a movement away from the stories of *either* total responsibility, such as individual grit, *or* of total lack of responsibility, such as genetic determinism. Because both of those types of stories place the individual at the center (see Rogers, Niwa, Chung, Yip, & Chae, 2021). If we move toward centering the collective, we move to a place where we tell new stories.

And this movement is a responsibility that falls heavy on psychologists. We need to understand how the intense emphasis on personal growth and change might be denying important realities, how we have not attuned to alternative hypotheses and theories in meaningful ways, how we have not been critical enough of the quality of our methods and our data about growth and change. If we really do care about positive, healthy change, if we really want to serve people, if we really want to be a part of meaningful cultural change, we need to change the stories we tell as a discipline.

I keep getting asked, "But don't you think it is possible to change?" That is the wrong question. The question needs to be "*Why* is it so hard to change?" Because change *is* possible. But considering the many obstacles to change—at the personal and collective levels—is imperative, and it is urgent, if we are to relieve the individual burden rising from the cultural value system that emphasizes personal responsibility.

PART II

The Data on Change

4

Evidence for Change From the Field of Personality Development

Traits, Attachment, and Posttraumatic Growth

Although I am most interested in the possibility of changing one's *identity*, there are insights to be gained from examining how researchers have approached the study of other kinds of change, and how those findings are or are not consistent with my larger argument. I will focus on three aspects of change found within the personality development literature: trait change, change in attachment representation, and change in the form of posttraumatic growth (touched on briefly in Chapter 2). This array also covers two levels of the broad construct of personality, of which narrative identity is the third level (e.g., McAdams & Pals, 2006).

McAdams (e.g., 1995) has argued that the first level of personality concerns traits, which are most often defined as the Big Five: Openness to Experience, Conscientiousness, Extraversion/Introversion, Agreeableness, and Neuroticism/Emotional Stability (e.g., John, Naumann, & Soto, 2008; McCrae & Costa, 2004). These traits are viewed to be relatively stable and partly heritable individual differences in thinking, feeling, and behaving (McCrae & Costa, 2008). Aspects of these traits are observable early in development as temperament (e.g., McAdams, 2015; Shiner &

DeYoung, 2013) and are relatively stable across the lifespan (e.g., Roberts & DelVeccio, 2000).

The second level of personality, according to McAdams (1995), is characteristic adaptations. These concern general orientations to the world, such as ways of thinking, characteristic ways of relating to others, and developmental concerns. I focus on two kinds of characteristic adaptations: attachment representations and outcomes of posttraumatic growth, such as character strengths like wisdom and compassion.

I choose these three aspects of personality because there has been decent empirical attention to whether and how they may change, and because these are constructs of interest to psychologists and laypeople alike. For example, decreasing one's level of neuroticism toward greater emotional stability may be a meaningful shift for persons (and for those with whom they are in relationships).

PERSONALITY TRAIT CHANGE

Despite the emphasis on stability in personality traits, theoretically there is room for some change. When thinking about change over time, there are traditionally two primary ways that personality scientists address this process. The first is *mean-level* change, an approach that focuses on whether a sample of participants shows change over time on average. The second approach is to look at *rank-order* stability and change. In this approach, researchers focus on whether people maintain their ranked place in the group on a particular characteristic compared to others in the sample over time. For example, if you are the most agreeable person in the sample at Time 1 and move down to the 10th spot in the sample at Time 2, changing your spot in the rank order, that suggests developmental movement. If you stay at the top of the pack on agreeableness at different assessment points, there is stability in that trait, at least relative to others.

Using these two approaches, the basic findings suggest modest mean level change for some traits at certain points in the lifespan, and remarkable stability in where people fall on the spectrum relative to each other over time (Roberts & Delvecchio, 2000). That is, there may be some average changes, but most people remain stable in comparison to others over time. Despite the modesty of these findings, scholars have put a lot of effort into examining the possibility of trait change, perpetuating the idea of the promise of such change.

The most prominent explanation for mean-level change comes from Brent Roberts's work on the Neo-Socioanalytic Model of Personality (e.g., Roberts & Nickel, 2021; Roberts & Wood, 2006; see also Hogan & Roberts, 2004). The most replicable and relatively robust findings show increases in agreeableness, conscientiousness, and emotional stability (i.e., decreases in neuroticism) in young and middle adulthood (e.g., Lucas & Donnellan, 2011; Roberts & Mroczek, 2008; Roberts, Walton, & Viechtbauer, 2006). So, basically, the good stuff gets better and the bad stuff gets less bad as we become adult community members, which Roberts more eloquently calls the *maturity principle* (see Klimstra & McLean, 2023, for a critique of this label). However, Roberts's explanation for these changes is not a humanistic vision of self-actualization. Rather, he argues that we develop to adapt successfully to meet specific culturally valued goals, in particular the goals of forming lasting relationships and work-related achievement (Hogan & Roberts, 2004). For example, increasing conscientiousness helps with doing well at work, and increasing agreeableness and decreasing neuroticism help in having good relationships. In other words, if we change at all, it is to better meet cultural demands. The reason I think this is important is because it suggests that any observed change may be driven by our need for cultural validation, acceptance, and belonging. In other words, understanding change may be more about understanding the collective, rather than the narrow focus on the individual.

In more recent work, Roberts (see Wrzus & Roberts, 2017) has focused on how this modest mean-level change might happen. He and his colleagues have focused on how repeated daily situations may move people toward trait change under the right conditions. These conditions include (1) experiencing "unpleasant self-discrepancy," (2) whether or not the change in characteristic is perceived to be important and desirable (in my words, culturally valued), and (3) whether the change is possible.

But the *coalescing* of these conditions is likely a rarity, and there are a lot of opportunities to jump off the change train, a lot of what they call "exit points," and other obstacles:

> there are many steps necessary for personality change to occur, whereas many "exit points" exist which may preclude change (see also Roberts, 2006; Roberts et al., 2008). These differences in paths leading to change and paths precluding change might explain why personality characteristics are often quite stable (i.e., do not change more) and why it is difficult to change characteristics, for instance, motivated by goals to change and during therapy. (Wrzus & Roberts, 2017, pp. 11–12)

They also note that explicit changes in self-representation may be less likely because of the press to maintain stability in self-views. Even if we desire change, we may have *more* of a desire to remain the same, to be predictable. Our almost total reliance on survey-based self-report measures as a field makes this nearly impossible to disentangle. In short, there are a lot of obstacles to change, and even if we do change, we may not characterize that change *as* change because of our desire to maintain stable self-views (a methodological conundrum, if you ask me).

And yet . . . there is a burgeoning literature on the phenomenon of intentionally trying to change, termed *volitional trait change*. That is, despite the obstacles to change articulated by Wrzus and Roberts, researchers in this area still have faith in the individual's ability to overcome them.

> People set goals, follow needs, strive for enhancement, select or avoid situations, and manipulate or create environmental conditions—*thus, people are often agents of their own stability and change* (Hennecke, Bleidorn, Denissen, & Wood, 2014). That is, although people cannot change their genetic makeup by choice, other personal and environmental sources are *subject to individual control*. (Wagner, Orth, Bleidorn, Hopwood, & Kandler, 2020, p. 2; emphasis in italics)

One of the main sources of data on volitional trait change comes from Nate Hudson's lab (e.g., Hudson, 2019), where he has found that most people he has sampled want to increase in socially desirable traits—become more conscientious, less neurotic, and more extroverted. He has found that when you ask people if they want to change particular traits, and then measure those traits over time, they show some change. However, his studies are fairly short (about 16 weeks), he samples primarily white college students in the United States (who are in a time of developmental change; e.g., Roberts & Delvecchio, 2000), and he finds fairly small levels of change, even for those who want to change the most. Finally, there are some concerns with the replicability of these results (see Hudson, Fraley, Chopik, & Briley, 2020; Robinson, Noftle, Gup, Asadi, & Zhang, 2015).

Even with some concerns about the reliability, replicability, and validity of these results, it seems like people can't get enough of the idea of the potential for change. And this idea is not only popular for those invested and interested in psychology. Scholars in the fields of public health, marketing, behavioral economics, and others argue that "self-nudges" can "enable people to design and structure their own decision environments—that is, to act as citizen choice architects" (Reijula & Hertwig, 2022, p. 1). Critically, these are not changes in personality traits. Self-nudges are situational behavioral changes, small reminders to do the right thing: putting the letters to be mailed next to the front door, or putting the veggies on the top shelf of the fridge so you won't forget to eat them. What is critical is that the idea that we can change part of how we act bleeds into the ideology that we can change other parts of ourselves, such as traits or identity, because it fits with the ideology of individual responsibility. And, of course, the emphasis is explicitly *not* on how policy changes might curb unhealthy behavior or increase healthy behaviors (e.g., limiting sugar in school lunches, increasing access to fresh produce through the Supplemental Nutrition Assistance Program), but on "self deployed control strategies" (Rejula & Hertwig, 2022, p. 3). When people fail . . . it is their fault. Not ours.

So despite the relatively modest data on trait and behavior change, data which are also compromised by sampling and design, there is still an emphasis on the possibility of change. This emphasis carries over to other disciplines and pervades many aspects of popular culture. To be clear, I am not saying that change is impossible or that behavioral regulation is not an important part of adaptation and healthy living. My concern is with the relentless messaging that focuses on the role of the individual in making change happen, particularly when that message comes from structural entities. For example, the emphasis that school districts place on the now highly questionable concepts of grit and growth mindset to improve children's performance is not only questionable based on the data (e.g., Burgoyne, Hambrick, & Macnamara, 2020; Credé, Tynan, & Harms, 2017; Li & Bates, 2019; Macnamara & Burgoyne, 2022; Ris, 2015), but it also enables an inattention to systemic change.

Thus, even though there is some change, for some people, in the direction of culturally desired characteristics, the study of personality trait change turns a relatively blind eye to the role of culture, context, and systems in that change (see also Klimstra & McLean, 2023). Perhaps one of the greatest failures of social science was our inability to impact behavioral change in the context of COVID-19. Although there are a lot of ways that academic psychology *can* contribute to understanding why some people would not take a vaccine—how misinformation is spread, how to nudge people in the direction of particular behaviors, and, yes, how stable and unbending belief systems and identities are—our inattention to systems is a serious downfall. Drawing attention to these individual characteristics and explanations may not actually be very helpful, because the best answer we have seen so far to curbing the pandemic was vaccine mandates—that is, structural change (Mills & Rüttenauer, 2022).

ATTACHMENT REPRESENTATIONS

Another critical domain of personality concerns the internalized schemas we have about our close and intimate relationships, or attachment representations. The premise of attachment theory is that our early exposure to and interaction with our primary caregivers provides a template for what to expect in intimate relationships. Bowlby, the theoretical architect of attachment theory (e.g., 1969; but see Ainsworth for the empirical life: e.g., Ainsworth, Blehar, Waters, & Wall, 1978; Bretherton, 1992), was clear that these representations are dependent on our early experiences and were likely stable and hard to change, in part because these schemas rest on prediction. We form schemas so we know what to expect under conditions of threat or, more specifically, to predict how our caregivers will respond to us in moments when we need them. Our ability to predict such behavior enables us to develop coping strategies to manage those situations of threat, coping patterns that become stable individual differences. The only way to really change these patterns, then, is through repeated changes in similar experiences (akin to the argument about repeated events and trait change; Wrzus & Roberts, 2017). For example, if one developed an insecure schema in childhood, repeatedly experiencing a caregiver as responsive to one's needs might move one toward a more trusting and secure orientation over time. But that can be hard to come by. In describing the challenge of changing attachment representations over time, Chris Fraley uses the concept of canalization, which captures how increasingly difficult it is to modify a cell the more it develops. Like a marble rolling down a slope, as it picks up speed, it is harder to change course (Fraley & Brumbaugh, 2004; Fraley, Gillath, & Deboeck, 2021; see also Khan, Chong, Theisen, Young, & Fraley, 2020).[1]

Despite the expectation of stability in attachment representations, there is an intriguing idea of the "earned secure" person. This is someone who experienced suboptimal attachment experiences in early development, resulting in feelings of insecurity in relationships and less effective strategies for managing threat (e.g., avoidance), but who finds security in an adult relationship in which they come to expect prompt and effective caregiving when needed (Roisman, Padrón, Sroufe, & Egeland, 2002; Saunders, Jacobvitz, Zaccagnino, Beverung, & Hazen, 2011). The data on this concept are hard to come by because the best test is to have

---

[1]. There is research on the importance of disrupting unhealthy caregiving patterns through *early* intervention—before attachment representations have had time to canalize (e.g., Shonkoff & Phillips, 2000; Thompson, 2004).

an assessment of attachment in infancy or early childhood, and then to follow those same people over time to see how they're doing in their adult relationships. Further, the likelihood of change is small, meaning that large samples are needed to reliably detect the phenomenon. There are several longitudinal studies of attachment, but the sample sizes are predictably low. For example, in one study that began with 267 infants, 170 were able to be followed as adults, and 30 met the requirements for prospectively assessed earned security (Roisman et al., 2002). Although this suggests it is possible to change attachment representations toward security, we don't know if the people who remained in the study are representative of the broader population. It is also hard to say much more than the possibility of change exists, because we can't conduct reliable statistical tests with such low numbers about potential explanations of such change.

In a different kind of analysis, Chris Fraley has examined change in self-reported attachment representations in adults in relation to a variety of life events experienced (Fraley et al., 2021). For example, is a break-up associated with change in one's attachment representations? Or an illness? One study included over 4,000 participants who experienced a range of different types of naturally occurring events, some but not all reasonably related to attachment (e.g., starting a new relationship versus changing jobs). Participants varied in the number of assessments and time spent in the study, but the average length of participation was 2 years, ranging from 6 months to over 3 years. Researchers found that there were some immediate changes to attachment representations subsequent to experiencing a major life event, but that most people reverted to their original score—meaning the changes were not particularly enduring. However, there were individual differences, with *some* people experiencing more enduring change—either becoming more secure or less secure, depending on how they interpreted the events they experienced.

So, again, we see modest change, for a few people. And as Fraley et al. acknowledge, there are several important limitations. First, there was a limited number of particular types of events that may have been particularly impactful (e.g., childbirth). The sample was predominantly white and female. The data were all self-report. And there were events, or processes, that were not measured that might help to explain the relatively minimal change that was observed, such as whether people entered therapy. That is, there was no assessment of external, or structural, supports that might constrain or facilitate change. This is interesting because even when structural elements are part of study design, they are often not part of analyses. For example, in the longitudinal study of earned security described earlier (Roisman et al., 2002), the sample was originally selected due to the position the mothers had in the socioeconomic system—they were under-resourced, poor, young, and receiving prenatal care at public health clinics. Yet that system was not a part of understanding how change in attachment representations might come about. None of these studies included systemic or structural variables in their analysis.

POSTTRAUMATIC GROWTH

In Chapter 2 I discussed the concept of posttraumatic growth in terms of its representation in a cultural master narrative of redemption. To refresh, the general concept in this literature is that, in the United States at least, most people say they have grown after experiencing trauma (see Frazier et al., 2009; Tedeschi & Calhoun, 1996). In support of evidence for the prevalence of such a narrative, Frazier et al. (2009) point to the ways such messages have been pushed by the American Psychological Association in a public education campaign called "The Road to Resilience." However, there is a major flaw in this line of research: until recently the bulk of the research was retrospective and self-report. That is, researchers asked people *after* they experienced adversity if they thought they had grown at all. What would you say? To be a good American, to give people the answer you know they want to hear, to live up to expectations, to be liked, to feel good about *yourself*, you'd say you had grown. This represents a measurement error at the highest level (Jayawickrime & Blackie, 2014; see also Blackie et al., 2023). We have no idea if we are measuring actual growth, desire to think one has grown, or a desire to meet cultural demands, some combination of the three, or something else entirely (see McLean et al., 2023, for a critique of the posttraumatic growth literature).

Like with the attachment research described above, there is a desperate need for prospective studies in the field of posttraumatic growth. And now we have some. Most of these newer studies focus on growth in what are called character strengths, aspects of personality at McAdams' level 2 that we think might develop after adversity (compassion, gratitude, etc.), and the current data are pretty clear. Across a fairly diverse set of samples, evidence for change following various types of adversity is weak at best (e.g., Blackie & McLean, 2022; Chopik et al., 2022; Frazier et al., 2009; Lamade et al., 2020; see also Chapter 2).

For example, Frazier et al. (2009) examined a large sample of undergraduates from four institutions over an 8-week period, some of whom experienced traumatic events during that time. They found several things that bear on the current discussion. First, the researchers found that *perceived* growth post-adversity was not correlated with measures of *actual* growth in relevant domains, such as gratitude. That is, reporting that you *think* you have grown is not related to assessments of whether you have *objectively* grown. They also observed objective change in only 25% of the sample, but these participants didn't *think* they had changed. This may reflect the self-continuity principle discussed by Roberts, in which there is a desire to maintain stability in self-views. This underscores the methodological challenge of relying only on self-report data.

In another example, Chopik et al. (2022) examined Army soldiers (n = 22,000–126,000 depending on the analysis) before and after their first deployment. They found that most soldiers were high in character strengths to begin with and remained so over time. A smaller group was low on character strengths and remained so over time. A still smaller group declined in levels of character strengths and generally rebounded to predeployment levels. There was no evidence of growth.

Finally, Lamade et al. (2020) examined change in character strengths after two terrorist attacks in Paris, with matched comparison samples from Australia and the United States. There were few observed changes, and those that were observed were quite small and seemingly random.

Again, these data show us that change, or in this case growth after adversity, is rare. Maybe it's the case that adversity can reveal strengths, but it doesn't necessarily create it.

METHODOLOGICAL CHALLENGES

In closing, I want to note that I have highlighted some methodological challenges in this chapter, such as the representativeness of the samples, the need for quite large samples, the concerns with data on self-reported change, and the need for prospective designs that assess the conditions under which change might happen. All of these studies examining change in relation to events are also compromised by lack of experimental control. That is, even when we see a relation between an event and change, we don't know whether the change is due to a particular event or not. This list is not meant to create total helplessness or hopelessness in the social scientist. It is meant to remind us of the humility we need to embody when we communicate what we know and what we don't know (see also Rogers et al., 2023).

Another issue not yet raised is the bias in our field for publishing statistically significant results and for discarding studies that produce no statistically significant results. This is sometimes referred to as the "file drawer problem" (e.g., Rosenthal, 1979). When we have data that don't show any significant findings, it is very hard to publish, leaving them in the "file drawer." In other words, for most of the history of empirical psychology, we had to have statistically significant results to publish a paper (e.g., Bakker, van Dijk, & Wicherts, 2012; Ferguson & Heene, 2012). Finding no difference between groups, for example, was not publishable. In terms of change, this means that if we find no statistically significant change over time, it would be very hard to publish. For many, a common practice was "p-hacking"—using inappropriate statistics or selective reporting to show a statistically significant result (see Friese & Frankenbach, 2020). For many, even most, this was not an intentionally deceptive practice, but rather the common practice of the day. But this resulted in scholars seeking to show change, for example, when there really was none in order to get a paper published. This means that we have no idea how many studies have shown no change that were never able to be published. I have some of my own failed (unpublished) interventions that were aimed at changing how people narrated the events of their lives (see Mansfield, Pasupathi, & McLean, 2022). To be clear, I deal with all of these issues in my own work, so I am not calling in these researchers in particular; these are issues we all face.

But when we continue to tell a story for which the data are lacking, we become part of the problem: We sustain particular, possibly damaging, cultural narratives for our community members. Our heavy investment in the ideas of growth and change may be because we are optimistic and hopeful beings and/or, with greater or lesser degrees of self-awareness, because our careers rest on these ideas. Either way we hold positions of authority and power, and we need to recognize our role in perpetuating particular narratives and ideologies, especially when the data are lacking.

Finally, although these data are useful in thinking about how we approach the study of change, they are not focused on identity—our central and fundamental understanding of who we are. Our identities may be even harder to change because we, and others, are more invested in them. In the next chapter, I examine the extant data.

5

Evidence for Change in Narrative Identity

The Case of Repeated Narration

Having looked at other types of change, I now turn to the data on change in narrative identity. To answer this question, I will focus primarily on longitudinal studies of *repeated narration*—studies in which the same individuals provide narratives at different points across time. The literature on repeated narration is small but growing. A good portion of the studies are descriptive, exploratory, and qualitative; there are few direct or conceptual replications at this point. The literature is also situated in different subfields (e.g., developmental, personality, cognitive), which means that the analyses are not always the same or fully comparable. So there are few definitive answers in this chapter. But the current state of the field gives us a lot of food for thought.

As with the research on trait change discussed in Chapter 4, there are several ways to examine repeated narration. The first is to examine *how* people narrate similar types of experiences over time. For example, I might ask someone to narrate a life low point and then again ask the same person for a low point 3 years later. The event narrated may or may not be the same, but I can look at whether someone uses the same narrative features in narrating low points. For example, when I tell the story of my father's death, I am likely to imbue the story with visceral details of the hospital room and the emotional complexities of experiencing grief and gratitude in the same moment. Each of these characteristics can be coded into concrete variables, such as factual and interpretive elements of the story, and emotional tone. I can then look to see whether I tell events from my miserable first year at college with similar kinds of features. If I do, then we could assume that I approach the narration of negative events in similar ways. In short, this kind of assessment has been used to get at *characteristic* ways of narrating experiences, regardless of whether it is the same event or not. This tells us more about a person's general way of interpreting and narrating the past, and less about the particularities of someone's life story.

The second way to examine repeated narration is to examine how the same event is narrated over time. In this case, I might ask someone for a life low point, and then ask that person to narrate that same event 3 years later—that is, how might I narrate the specific story of my father's death at two different time points? Although this is a very direct test of story change, this comes with complications. First, repeatedly asking people to narrate the same event likely changes the narrative of the event; the study procedures become an intervention (Syed, Juan, & Juang, 2011; see also Pasupathi & Wainryb, 2019). We also don't know if the events we ask people to renarrate continue to be particularly important and meaningful. That is, the low point at Time 1 may not be central to a person's identity anymore at Time 2, so we can't be sure if the change in narration means anything about their identity.

With awareness of these methodological challenges, the main question I had in reviewing the literature was what the study of repeated narration tells us about whether and how people can change their stories. In this chapter I examine both *how* people narrate events over time, as well as how *specific events* are renarrated. Even with the data being fairly nascent, I do see a few commonalities in results that span different methods, theoretical approaches, and types of data, which I hope will be useful in thinking about identity and story change.

DO WE CHANGE *HOW* WE TELL STORIES OVER TIME?

As with research on personality trait development (Chapter 4), researchers have examined both mean-level and rank-order change in the ways that people narrate events. However, the bulk of the longitudinal studies examining mean-level change have been conducted in childhood, adolescence, and emerging adulthood, stages in which we would expect change due to cognitive development and the cultural demands for identity work. And the extant work does suggest evidence of a developmental maturity akin to Roberts's maturity principle on trait development, with longitudinal studies showing increases in aspects of narration such as autobiographical reasoning and coherence from childhood through emerging adulthood (Köber, Schmiedek, & Habermas, 2015; McAdams et al., 2006; Reese et al., 2011). In other words, youth increasingly hone their skills at interpreting past events with rich detail, elaboration, and meaning, developing stories that are consistent with culturally valued ways of narration.

In terms of rank-order analyses, recall that here we are looking at how people keep their rank relative to other people. If I tell a story with the highest score for negative emotional tone at Time 1, do I maintain my rank at Time 2, still telling a story with the highest negativity relative to others in the sample?

In two of the landmark studies on repeated narration in terms of *how* we tell stories, we see evidence for substantial stability. In one of the first studies to examine repeated narration, Thorne, Cutting, and Skaw (1998) collected relationship memory narratives from emerging adults at two time points, 6 months apart. The feature of narrative that they focused on was the kind of motive expressed in memory narratives, which they found was quite similar across time, regardless of the story told. That is, if I express a need for intimacy in narrating a past relationship event, I am likely to do so the next time I narrate a relationship event, regardless of whether it is the same event.

In the next landmark study, McAdams et al. (2006) collected life story scenes (e.g., low point, turning point) at time points of 3 months and 3 years apart from college students. This team also found substantial rank-order stability in how participants told stories, such as the emotional tone of their stories. The stability coefficients were actually similar to rank-order stability in personality traits. More recently, McLean, Dunlap, Jennings, Litvitskiy, and Lilgendahl (2021) found similar scores on rank-order stability in exploratory processing across 4 years of emerging adulthood (see also Bauer, Tasdemir-Ozdes, & Larkina, 2014; Booker, Fivush, & Graci, 2021; Mitchell, 2021; Waters, Köber, Raby, Habermas, & Fivush, 2019). Those who were very exploratory in narrating past events at Time 1 continued to be so, compared to others, across the assessments. Overall, these studies suggest that individuals may have characteristic ways of telling stories that persist through time and across different types of stories.

It is important to note, however, that not all studies show remarkable stability, and some of this depends on both the feature of narrative scholars are examining and the type of event. For example, McLean et al. (2021) found different levels of rank-order stability depending on the feature of narrative. They found lower rank-order stability for self-event connections than for exploratory processing. Exploratory processing captures general ways that individuals reflect on important events in their lives (e.g., Pals, 2006), so it makes sense that there is more stability in this aspect of narration. Self-event connections concern the ways we link particular events to our understanding of self, such as whether the event reveals something negative or positive about us (Pasupathi et al., 2007), so the type of event might matter more for how we narrate it rather than something stable about us that causes us to narrate events in the same way.

Similarly, in a related area of study on intra-individual variability in how we narrate the past, researchers have examined not change over time, but change in how individuals narrate different types of events at one point in time. For example, if I tell one story with an elaborative and meaning-laden insight I gained in going through a break-up, am I likely to do that with a story about a fight with a friend? Or do the particular events draw out different types of narrative strategies? Here we see that the type of event is actually quite important, often more important, in determining how we narrate it than are characteristics of the person narrating it (McLean et al., 2017; McLean, Syed, & Shucard, 2016; Pasupathi et al., 2020).

This variability in how we narrate events suggests that some narrative strategies may be more appropriate for certain events than others. For example, resolution would be a pretty irrelevant feature for telling the happy story of meeting one's partner, where there was nothing to fix or no negative emotions to ameliorate. A disruptive story of learning that one's partner had cheated calls more for an explanation of how it ended—did you stay together or not? That is, we wouldn't expect people to use resolution in narrating all events, only in some. In contrast, the degree of coherence one expresses in narrating events should be more stable across events because coherence is a developmental skill used to communicate one's past more or less clearly. If I am not very good at providing enough detail so that audiences can understand the story, that goes for most stories I narrate. In fact, we do see more consistency in scores on coherence across events compared to features like resolution (McLean et al., 2017; Waters et al., 2019). The role of event type in understanding individual differences in the consistency of narration is a new, potentially fruitful, and highly complex area of study (Pasupathi et al., 2020).

In short, the data on characteristic ways of narration suggest that there are developmental changes in childhood, adolescence, and emerging adulthood consistent with growing abilities at narration and the demand to do so. In emerging adulthood, we see that many aspects of narration show rank-order stability. Given the data on intra-individual variability, it is worth asking whether that stability may depend in part on the type of event we are narrating (e.g., positive or negative) or the aspect of narrative we are examining (coherence or resolution).

DO WE CHANGE HOW WE NARRATE *PARTICULAR* STORIES OVER TIME?

The data on specific events are fewer and harder to interpret, because of the limitations mentioned earlier: (1) asking people to repeatedly narrate the same event might change the story of the event, and (2) we don't know if the events we are asking people to repeat are still actually important to them. In Table 5.1 I have displayed the existing studies in which researchers have

Table 5.1 Event Repetition

Developmental Stage	Adolescents	Adults	Emerging Adults	Emerging Adults	Midlife Adults
Timeline	4–8 years	6 years	6 months	18 months	3 years
Prompt	7 Most Important Memories	1 Relationship-Defining Memory	13 Relationship Memories	1 Ethnicity-Related Memory	12 Key Life Story Scenes
% Repeated	3%–25%	11%	12%	18%	27%
Authors	Köber & Habermas, 2017	Mackinnon et al., 2016	Thorne et al., 1998	Syed & Azmitia, 2010	Adler (2019)

Developmental Stage	Emerging Adults	Emerging Adults	Adolescents	Adults	Adults
Timeline	3 months; 3 years	1–4 years	4 years	3–9 months	4 years
Prompt	10 Key Life Story Scenes	4 College Transition Memories	1 Earliest Memory	4 Relationship Transgression Memories	1 Earliest Memory
% Repeated	23%; 17%	20%	20%	27%	82%
Authors	McAdams et al. 2006	Patterson et al. 2022	Reese & Robertson, 2019	Blackie & McLean (unpublished data)	Bauer et al., 2014

Developmental Stage	Adolescents	Adolescents	Emerging Adults		
Timeline	1 year	2 weeks	3 months		
Prompt	1 Turning Point Memory	7 Most Important Memories	5 Current Relationship Memories		
% Repeated	27%	50%–65%	70%		
Authors	Mitchell, 2021	Köber & Habermas, 2017	Drivdahl & Hyman, 2014		

asked participants for narrative repetition in some form, with at least two time points. But the studies in Table 5.1 primarily ask people to respond to open prompts (e.g., life story low point), rather than specific events (e.g., earliest memory, wedding day), meaning that people do not have to tell the exact same story each time we ask them. The percentages represent how many people *do* repeat the same event, which is not many: Most people do *not* tell the same story over time. I have laid the table out so that the percent of repeated memories moves from lowest to highest.[1] My read of the basic findings is that the highest level of repeated stories comes from studies that have a very short time frame of highly important, very specific events, or currently relevant events.[2] Even if the repetition of specific events is relatively low, I offer four speculations about the data.

Speculation 1: Repetition as Stagnation

In thinking about event repetition, the question often asked is whether it is useful or healthy to repeat the same things. My first speculation is that event repetition, telling the same story, may indicate a kind of stuck-ness, or rigidity, in one's identity development. In support of this speculation, Syed and Azmitia (2010) found that college students who narrated the same experience related to their ethnicity 18 months apart scored higher on a measure of identity foreclosure, or a lack of exploration of identity, compared to those who narrated different events. Interestingly, Mitchell (2021) asked adolescents to narrate a turning-point narrative 1 year apart and found that those who repeated the same event had higher life satisfaction than nonrepeaters. This could represent a contentment that comes when one is not experiencing the challenges of exploration (see also

---

1. Some papers reported *people* who repeated narratives, rather than the percent of repeated memories, if there are more than two time points, which are not reported here (e.g., Josselson, 2000).

2. Except Blackie and McLean (unpublished data), but those were not all highly important, thus not always remembered. Reese and Roberston (2019) is an interesting exception; it was collected during a time when participants' life stories were still forming.

Eriksson, McLean, & Frisén, 2020), although that is a rather speculative interpretation that needs empirical follow-up.

Speculation 2: Repetition as Exploration

The second speculation is that repetition might instead represent continued exploration, rather than rigidity. Several qualitative studies have used case studies to examine how people narrate the same events over time and have seen evidence of continued exploration of especially important life events. For example, McLean, Köber, and Haraldsson (2019) examined the case of one woman who repeated several events in her life story interview 3 years apart, but the stories continued to evolve as she examined their relevance to new and developing events. Similarly, Josselson (2009) found that one woman who repeated a specific story about a romantic relationship in emerging adulthood at several time points across 35 years made meaning of the event in different ways depending on her current developmental concerns. She was able to use the story to understand different aspects of herself made salient at different life stages (see also Mischler, 2004), such as in her role as a young woman seeking love, her role as a wife in midlife, and her role as a mother to a daughter just beginning to explore her own identity. "Like a kaleidoscope, the same elements are recombined to show a different pattern, all in the service of the dominant selves of the moment" (Josselson, 2009, pp. 661–662). These limited data suggest that whether repetition signals rigidity or deeper exploration, and for whom, are questions worthy of more pointed study.

Speculation 3: Repetition as Importance

The third speculation is that events may be repeated because they are just really important to one's identity. In her study of repeated turning points in an adolescent sample, Mitchell (2021) found that the most frequent theme of repeated events was death of very close others, such as parents, grandparents, or best friends. Such events are likely highly salient and shape one's thinking about one's own life story (see also McLean et al., 2019). This issue of salience may also explain the repeated events in short time frames or of very specific events (e.g., earliest memory) that are in a kind of permastore in one's memory bank.

Speculation 4: Repetition Signals Culturally Valued Stories

The fourth speculation, and most relevant to the larger arguments I have been making, is that those who have more repeated events are more likely to align with cultural master narratives of what a life story should look like than those who repeat stories less. In our case study analysis of high and low repeaters (McLean et al., 2019), we found that high repeaters had more "life script" events (Berntsen & Rubin, 2004), or events that are considered normative or culturally expected (e.g., graduation from school, marriage, having a child), than did low repeaters. Mitchell (2021) found the same thing in her analysis of high and low repeaters. This is notable given the difference in life stage for these two studies (midlife versus adolescence) and time span (1 year vs. 3 years). Similarly in a lifespan sample, Köber and Habermas (2017) found that normative life events predicted life story stability over time.

Again, these data pointing to the role of master narratives in narrative repetition are few and largely descriptive and qualitative, but they do speak to some interesting ideas. Moin Syed and I proposed that biographical master narratives serve as a schema for how to tell one's life story, including what events are important to include (see also Berntsen & Rubin, 2004). From a master narrative perspective, including these events in one's life story is expected, even demanded, and rewarded. It makes sense that such a press and a validation would make those events easier and more likely to be recalled (see also Demorest, Popovska, & Dabova, 2012; Patterson et al., 2022; Singer et al., 2013). This is consistent with the research on normative trait change (Roberts & DelVecchio, 2000), in which mean-level trait change might be an indication of conforming to societal expectations (see also Eriksson et al., 2020).

Importantly, when people repeat these culturally expected stories in their own life stories, this is not a simple individual choice. This is an internalization (likely passive) of cultural expectations, an internalization that serves to uphold the master narratives that privilege certain people, such as those who are married and educated. This is not to shame those who find their wedding day to be important to their identity, but to acknowledge the role that stories—personal and cultural—play in maintaining systems of power and privilege.

SPECULATIONS ON WHAT THE EXISTING EVIDENCE TELLS US ABOUT IDENTITY CHANGE

These data tell us something about how narration changes over time. For example, overall, the existing data show that over time, we see little repetition of the same story. When we *do* see repetition, it may signal developmental processes (rigidity or exploration), and it may also signal the personal and cultural importance of particular stories. I think we can also tentatively say that the *way* we narrate those events appears to be fairly stable across time, given the data on rank-order stability. This is consistent with Piaget's conception of cognitive development in that, over time, we are more likely to assimilate new information into existing schemas, rather than to accommodate existing schemas to fit new information (Piaget & Inhelder, 1969).

These data do not provide overwhelming evidence for *identity change*—changing how you see yourself across time, context, and within a culture. Because they are limited in number, and have design challenges, and so on, it is pretty hard to come to firm conclusions. But I offer some speculations on two potential trajectories of identity change, with the caveat that I still think change is likely to be quite hard to come by.

Change by Degrees

First, if people experience a nudge toward a different interpretation of a story, perhaps through therapy or the questions or validations from a new audience, over time we might see that nudge begin to spill to other events, which *could* result in larger movement. I think of this kind of change as a *Two-Degrees Trajectory*, calling to mind an ocean liner nudged off course by two degrees. If it maintains that slight change in direction over many thousands of miles, the endpoint is quite different than it would have been had the ship stayed on its original trajectory. I'll offer one of my favorite narratives I have collected to probe the idea. The following is a self-defining memory narrative collected from an emerging adult:

> I was painting a huge picture of Santa Claus with my dad that he had cut out and we were going to put on the roof. I just remember how wonderful it felt to be spending time with just him and I was so happy and content. It was one of my happiest memories from childhood. The real shaping of it didn't happen until about two years ago. My dad was talking to me and remembering painting with me and he laughed to remember how stoned he was that day. I was so incredibly shocked. I had known he used to do all sorts of drugs, but I never thought he did them after I was born. It really made me go through and relook at my memories and see how there's so many things behind a situation that you never see. Things are not always as they seem. I told my mom about it and she was just surprised as hell to know that I didn't know about his drug use.

Although this person reports that she was "incredibly shocked," it is unlikely that she had a dramatic and sudden change in her identity. At the time of the event, some efforts to make meaning of the experience and how it might change her understanding of herself would be needed—there would be work to do. So what I see here is an *opportunity* for change. We do not know if this "relooking" results in substantive change for how she sees herself. But if over time as she includes this new story in her larger life story, repeating it, we might see a new shade to her identity. Perhaps she begins to hold a different interpretation of her relationship with her father, which changes some ways that she views her childhood, how she developed, and who she is now. Maybe she begins to trace some current psychological challenges to these newly visible childhood experiences. Maybe these current psychological challenges become more prominent in how she views herself.

But she also might not engage in much "relooking." It might be too challenging to change the story of her childhood, as well as her view of her relationship with her father. Perhaps her motivation to maintain the status quo as "good enough" overrides the effort of reinterpretation. She also might not have the right audience to explore such a change. And perhaps the available master narratives about how we are supposed to story our family relationships don't fit with her potential new interpretations of her family. It is also possible that she soon realizes that parents are people too, and it just isn't a big deal. The new story gets assimilated into the old story, and the weight of the revelation lessens as she is able to return to her original interpretations of her childhood and relationships.

There is no work of which I am aware that examines this two-degrees-type trajectory of repeated narration in relation to identity change. But there is one study that does provide some evidence of the potential for how this might work. Jon Adler (2012) examined participants who were undergoing 12 weeks of therapy. He examined weekly narratives about their thoughts and feelings about the therapeutic experience. Over the course of the 12-week study, he found that those who told increasingly more agentic stories showed improvements in their symptoms. Importantly, the way that they narrated their weekly stories preceded changes in their symptoms, suggesting that narration is a mechanism of change. However, there was no outcome variable of identity change, or even long-term change. We don't know what impact this increasing agency had on how they evaluated other parts of themselves, whether this new kind of narration spilled into other kinds of events, or whether it persisted once therapy was complete. Further, these people were arguably experiencing a pretty intensive support for changing their narration in the therapeutic context. They had a welcoming audience, time to practice new ways of narration, and a supportive scaffold for exploring this change. This study holds promise as a model for examining change over time, but the empirical design additions needed to understand actual identity change are not small.

As I hope is becoming clear, the methodological challenges of collecting data on repeated narration are serious, and we also need a massive amount of narrative data over a substantially long period of time to address questions of identity change. This is not impossible, but legitimately challenging. We would need large samples of people who have narratives like the young woman with the Santa Claus story to be followed over time, and we would need to collect a lot of narrative data from each person to see how potential reinterpretations might slowly spread to other stories. And, of course, I would argue that any study designed to test this would need to pay attention to the structural and cultural obstacles to these shifts, rather than assuming individual agency over interpretation and reinterpretation.

Seismic Change

A second possible trajectory that I propose is the *Seismic Trajectory*.[3] Rather than the slow-paced two-degrees trajectory, this is a trajectory in which something sudden and dramatic happens that may prompt major identity work, or an accommodation. The timescale may still be long, even similar to the two-degrees trajectory, in terms of reaching an "endpoint" of reasoning about the event and the self. But the push toward restorying is much more abrupt and unexpected, and likely more challenging and threatening. And such an experience may also *demand* change or at least attention—both from the person experiencing the disruption to identity and from the larger culture that might expect a story about what happened and what it means.

In one of the few lines of research on such a possibility, we come back to Jon Adler (Adler, 2018; Adler et al., 2019), who has examined how people who suddenly acquire disabilities in adulthood understand their identities. These data are not repeated narratives, as the data were collected after the

---

3. See Miller (2004) for a discussion of "quantum" change, an idea that has a long (if relatively empirically unsupported) history in psychology (James, 1902).

seismic change (the methodological hurdles of anticipating who will experience a seismic change are obvious), but the data are instructive. In one study, Adler's team (2019) interviewed 13 people who had acquired a disability rather abruptly (e.g., sudden blindness, paralysis, amputation), to get at dramatic movement rather than a slower course of adjustment over time.

The acquisition of disability poses a profound challenge to multiple types of integration: who one is/was before and after the event, how one now fits in across various contexts, and how one understands oneself as a member of a new group (i.e., people with disabilities; see also Adler et al., 2022). Indeed, one of the primary findings from Adler's team was that all of their participants found that their acquired disability was an identity threat and a challenge for identity integration. Of course, integration can involve assimilating the new identity into the old one, or changing one's identity to accommodate what's new.

In terms of potential identity change, about half of the participants felt they were the same, and half felt they had changed. Some readers might attend more to the change findings, thinking: Of course, people changed! And, in fact, half of them did. Others might attend more to the other half of the sample: Wow, after such a profound event, half the people did *not* think they had changed! Given the nature of this challenge and disruption to identity, *I* find it somewhat remarkable that half of the participants felt they had not changed at all. It may be emblematic of and evidence for the press for identity stability and continuity.

The researchers also found that some participants were more actively engaged in reasoning about whether they had changed or not. Sometimes the process of autobiographical reasoning resulted in perceptions of change, but not always. In fact, for some, this reasoning resulted in feelings of sameness or continuity: "After working so hard at all this change, I finally feel more myself than I've ever felt" (Adler et al., 2019, p. 16). This is an excellent example of how one can experience profound change and still narrate the self as continuous through time, a tool of narrative autobiographical reasoning (Pasupathi et al., 2007).

Finally, for those who engaged in heavy reasoning and experienced an identity change, there was a notable trend of integrating the newly acquired disability with their identities in ways that were consistent with a cultural master narrative of growth. That is, when change was experienced, it was likely to be in the direction of cultural expectation—just like with trait change, posttraumatic growth, or repeated narration. The change we observe (and there may certainly be change that we are not observing or attending to) appears to be in the direction of meeting cultural demands. This, of course, makes me question the degree of latitude people have in storying themselves, and how much our stories are actually about the need or desire to belong.

To be clear, I do not want to dismiss or downplay the narratives of growth reported by these participants. This kind of reasoning is hard, meaningful work. The personal stories in this paper are profound. For many, this work appears to have resulted in stories that sustain and even uplift these individuals, and perhaps their families and loved ones who are inspired and humbled by their experiences. And there is also a master narrative at play that might facilitate this kind of autobiographical reasoning that centers on growth, and that might allow these people, and their stories, to experience more validation.

For those who want to tell a different kind of story of change, there may be a different set of challenges. Indeed, one participant who did not perceive identity change actively resisted the master narrative of redemption, and described its toxicity.

> The people who say, "Oh, you can do anything you did before if you just set your mind to it," Oh, pfft, please. And then, you know, there's the Dancing with the Stars, the snowboard star, you know, the fabulous amputees? Tired of all of them. You know, I feel like if, if I can do the regular things that is a major triumph. . . . You know those people who say, "Oh, cancer made me a better person," I'm sorry. I'm sorry. I didn't need this in any way. (Adler et al., 2021, p. 21)

For this participant, the master narrative of growth appears suffocating (see McLean et al., 2023). It may even limit her ability to fully explore the meaning of this event in her life, or to create a story that feels authentic to her experience, or to tell a story about the systemic challenges she faces as a person with an acquired disability. I wonder if she has been able to find anyone to hear and validate her story, outside of this research context.

THE CONTEXT OF IDENTITY CHANGE

Clearly, I think we need to understand how these larger contexts play critical roles in whether and how people experience change. In this paper on acquired disability, Adler et al. (2021) do an excellent job of describing their participants' negotiation with their own experiences and master narratives. I applaud their integration of the disability literature with the psychological literature—this is exactly the kind of work for which I am advocating because other disciplines, like disability studies, know how to center systems and structures better than we do in psychology (e.g., Davis, 2017; Garland Thomson, 2013). Adler and colleagues write that this approach is "grounded in an anti-individualist epistemology that regards the individual as embedded within dynamic and reciprocal social contexts that give rise to identity" (p. 2). The more of this kind of work we do, the more we expand the landscape of our understanding of human functioning and development in the structures and systems in which we live.

But I admit that one of the hardest jobs, perhaps especially for psychologists, is balancing the personal story on the one hand, and the role of systems and structure on the other. I recently listened to a story on the *On Point* podcast about the invisible epidemic of traumatic brain injury (TBI) in survivors of interpersonal violence (Sutherland & Chakrabarti, 2022). That is, when people are battered, they experience a phenomenon we typically associate with football players. Over the course of the podcast, the host and her guests paid a lot of attention to the structural obstacles to obtaining treatment for TBI, doing research on TBI, and even just to the lack of awareness of this epidemic. Most people have not heard of TBI in survivors of interpersonal violence. This is likely because most doctors don't screen for it, let alone diagnose it. Most funders won't provide resources for research because they say we have enough data on football players. This is despite the fact the population of patients for victims of interpersonal violence is quite different than football players (primarily women vs. men), and TBI can come from different experiences (e.g., getting knocked by a helmet vs. strangulation), both of which point to the need for more research on this epidemic. I found the interweaving of the personal and the systemic in the podcast to be remarkable, and the description of systemic obstacles to diagnosing and treating to be thorough and convincing.

But statistics and facts alone do not make for the most compelling of podcasts, and so the host did what many do—she included a personal story from a guest to bring the topic to life. She interviewed a survivor who told her story of abuse and repeated brain injury, and it is horrific. At the end, however, the survivor talked about her current life—she is safe, happy, and strong. It is a good story. I imagine that it is true to her. But the guests on the podcasts were persistent in emphasizing how important it was that people hear about the structural nature of the epidemic, such as obtaining diagnoses, treatment, and funding, not to mention patriarchal systems that keep interpersonal violence behind closed doors. And I couldn't help but wonder what the listener takes away. How much does the ending of the story matter? There is a sense of resolution for this one woman—she is ok. She is telling her story for the greater good. It is almost heroic. And does the personal story of redemption slide so nicely into our storied expectations that it calms the anger and the anguish over the structural obstacles she faced? That is, does her redemption story allow us to turn away from the system?

Again, I am not attempting to dismiss the stories our participants tell us. I am asking us to look at them, to hear them, in a different way. To use a different lens for interpreting the data. If we view her resolution and redemption not just as her own personal process of meaning-making but also as a mechanism for upholding the status quo, the implications of our analyses are quite different. One action scientists take is to choose the lens of analysis and to emphasize certain components of our data over others (see Rogers et al., 2023). Understanding the intimacy of the relationship among personal stories, cultural stories, and systems and structures is critical if we are to understand the full breadth and depth of human functioning from a psychological perspective.

PART III

Special Concerns

6

Transgressions as an Opportunity for Change?

One aspect of identity change that I have not discussed thus far is motivation for change. In the studies on volitional trait change discussed in Chapter 4, people wanted to change aspects of their personalities. When people go to therapy, it is assumed that there is a desire for change. The participants in Adler et al.'s (2021) study on acquired disability discussed in Chapter 5 experienced an event that demanded attention in terms of identity. In fact, their data suggest that events that *force* a consideration of change may be the best place to explore the possibility and trajectory of change. Another place that may be quite fruitful for understanding change is not when events happen *to* people, but when people play a causal role in the event: when they have violated cultural norms and expectations with their own actions.

Transgressions may provide motivation to change because the self has done harm, which may open up opportunity to transform into a self who will not harm again. There is also a culturally valued narrative template for change after committing a transgression—redemption in the form of atonement. But some complexities arise from transgressions too. Indeed, an individual story of atonement for transgressing is likely to limit attention to needed structural change because atoning appears to solve the problem: Responsibility has been taken for the action—nothing more to see here. And, paradoxically, despite the opportunity for change and the available template, there is relatively little engagement with transgressions in ways that might produce identity change. It turns out people don't want to think about their transgressions much. Finally, and of course, transgressions always have two parties—the perpetrator *and* the victim[1]—and the available templates and opportunities for change are quite different for these two parties. In unpacking these issues, I address transgressions broadly, though I draw special attention to the quite weighty transgressions of interpersonal violence, where I have focused some of my recent research.

Although we all commit relatively minor transgressions with frequency, larger transgressions can threaten the very heart of our personhood (Pasupathi & Wainryb, 2010). There is a substantial philosophical literature on identity that focuses on the importance of one's morals, values, and commitments as defining our identities (e.g., Ricour, 1992; see also Pasupathi, 2015; Pasupathi & Wainryb, 2010), or what Charles Taylor (1989) calls "orientation towards the good." As social animals, our need to be a part of a group and connect with others means that we need shared understandings and values about how to be a good person, however that is defined in the culture in which we are living. When we transgress, violating our orientations and commitments, there can be a desire to repair our relationships and ourselves, as well as to mitigate the chance that we'll do it again (see Pasupathi & Wainryb, 2010). However, despite the threats that transgressions can pose to our identities and social standing, the existing data suggest that we will do all sorts of mental gymnastics to *resist* engaging with the meaning of our transgressions in ways that might engender substantial change.

There are two main pathways for managing transgressions—dismiss them or else engage in reasoning about what they might mean for who we are. In terms of the former, we know that people don't often share their

---

1. The labels of "victim" and "survivor" are contested, political, and complex (e.g., Williamson & Serna, 2018). There are sound arguments for using each of these terms, arguments against using them, and arguments for different terms altogether. I have generally elected to use "victim" here to highlight the disparity in roles when comparing victims and perpetrators.

stories of transgressions, in part because of the fear of audience response and the shame they produce (Pasupathi et al., 2007, 2015; Thorne, McLean, & Dasbach, 2004). Since story*telling* is a process of narrative and identity development (e.g., McLean et al., 2007), *not* sharing transgression stories is certainly a good way to disengage from them, allowing us to forget or compartmentalize them, preserving oneself as good and negating the need for change.

Even when transgressions are told, preservation of self can still be at play. When transgressions are shared, it is likely that they are narrated as distanced from the self (Baumeister, Stillwell, & Wotman, 1990). *It was so unlike me to steal the watch, cheat on the test, lie to my girlfriend.* In this way transgressions can be viewed as a bad act, rather than the mark of a bad self, which means that fundamental change is not necessary. For some, transgressions can be shared in ways that suggest personal growth and learning (e.g., Lilgendahl, McLean, & Mansfield, 2013; Pasupathi & Wainryb, 2010). Yet whether that growth is indicative of identity change has not been assessed. Given the threat to self that comes with substantial change, my hunch is that, for *most* people, narrative engagement with transgressions, if there is any, is more about repair or restoration to the self prior to the transgression rather than change to a different self (see also Perlin & Fivush, 2021, for discussion of two kinds of redemption).

TRANSGRESSIONS AND FUNDAMENTAL CHANGE

When we shift the frame from the relatively common transgressions that we all commit to those that are much weightier—such as violent acts and serious harm to others—the demand for self-reflection and narration may be a little different. Such acts bring the possibility of "moral fragmentation" (Wainryb, 2011), creating the need for a story about how one has *fundamentally changed*, how one is no longer the person who committed those acts (Maruna, 2001; Maruna & Ramsden, 2004). Such "core change" may be the only solace to the self and others that the act will not happen again (Vesey, Martinez, & Christian, 2009). But this potential story of transformation and change may have varied consequences depending on whether the outcome we are looking at is within the perpetrator, the victim, or the larger society. We'll start with the perpetrator and society.

Transgression Stories: The Perpetrator Perspective

There is a very clear master narrative for those who have transgressed and desire re-entry into mainstream society: accountability, remorse, and growth. This may sound familiar: it is a kind of redemption, termed "atonement" (McAdams & Manczak, 2015). There are several necessary ingredients for atonement, perhaps most important the admission of wrongdoing and the acknowledgment of harm, as well as the making of reparations (Cerulo & Ruane, 2014; Delker et al., under review; McAdams & Manczak, 2015). Atonement embodies not a one-off apology, but a meaningful shift in self-understanding that promises against future harm (see Brennan, Swartout, Cook, & Parrott, 2018; Nigro, Ross, Binns, & Kurtz, 2020).

There are also specific forms of atonement popular among particular groups who have transgressed. Maruna, Wilson, and Curran (2006) discuss the available master narratives for religious conversion in prison as well as in Alcoholics Anonymous, narratives that rely heavily on atonement. Such narratives include taking full responsibility, not making excuses, and creating a new identity—essentially, being born again (Ramsden & Maruna, 2004). "This narrative reconstruction can be understood as a prototypical form of 'shame management'—helping outcast groups overcome their stigmatization and realign themselves with mainstream society" (Maruna & Ramsden, 2004, p. 130). And the available models, such as the redemption narrative found in Alcoholics Anonymous, suggest that this meaningful shift takes continued effort and practice to maintain: to "keep working the program." In short, *if* the perpetrator can pull it off, there are guidelines for revising oneself that are likely to be culturally accepted and validated, perhaps even celebrated (Snyder, 2019).

There are also recent data showing that such a narrative is positively evaluated by others. In a vignette-based study, my colleagues and I found that in narratives in which a perpetrator atoned for sexual violence, that perpetrator was seen as having more positive personality traits and was more likely to elicit empathy, compared to a perpetrator who did not atone (Delker et al., under review). Of course, atonement does not necessarily mean identity change, and we did not measure that in the vignette study. But atonement certainly may be a pathway toward change.

Although atonement may be a pathway to change, the template of atonement, as with any master narrative, can be rigid and constraining.

> Scholars consider storytelling among ex-offenders as potentially transformative and potentially oppressive. Restorative justice proponents view the exchange of stories as healing (Sullivan and Tifft 2001), yet others view the discourse of restorative justice as a new measure of controlling the socially marginalized (Arrigo and Schehr 1998). So-called twelve-step programs encourage self-described addicts to share rather scripted stories with one another (Denzin 1987; O'Reilly 1997; Swora 2002), but the tale of redemption can nonetheless provide a template for a desisting identity (Maruna 2001). In correctional treatment programs based on highly regarded cognitive models, facilitators monitor and edit ex-offenders' stories, urging speakers to adopt certain discourses about why they offended and how they might avoid re-offending (Fox 1999; Waldram 2007). In short, for ex-offenders, telling one's story promises a new start even as it invites a new sort of surveillance. (Presser & Kurth, 2009, p. 75)

Although this heavy press for conformity may help some to work their way through and out of a damaged identity, the required template may also stifle true engagement with and reflection on the event (see also Schneider & Wright, 2004, for a discussion of the role of denial). An uncomfortable part of thinking about these issues is the question of whether the atonement story is "true" or not. The field of narrative identity relies on subjective reports, and we privilege and value the voices of participants;

questioning authenticity is not part of the deal. But in these cases where change has such real-world consequences, the pressure for particular stories leaves open the risk of conformity without transformation; telling the right story, but not living it. The cultural press might result in inauthentic stories that do *not* prevent future harm and that do not truly signify transformation.

Transgression Stories: Societal Implications

And we, as a society, are complicit in this press for cultural alignment. A story of redemptive atonement restores order in the world because we have an explanation for one person's behavior and a promise of change. It allows us to move on and to realign with the predictable status quo. Indeed, in the vignette study mentioned earlier (Delker et al., under review), the more atonement that perpetrators expressed, the more raters viewed them as being responsible for the assault. One person's redemptive story of individual responsibility may make us less motivated to question other causes for this behavior, such as systemic roots of oppression and inequality that might play a larger role than we want to admit in the perpetration of transgressions. So just as stories about "bad seeds" allow us to ignore systems, so too do stories about those who have transformed. Either way—we are looking at persons, not structures and systems.

Further, we may place *more* responsibility and pressure for change on those who are structurally marginalized (e.g., Maruna et al., 2006; Victor & Waldram, 2015). For example, those who are incarcerated are disproportionately on the margins by virtue of race, ethnicity, and class. Once incarcerated, correctional programming (like the discipline of psychology itself) is built on a medical model of fixing the symptoms as though there is simply a deficit in the person, rather than the system (Veysey et al., 2009; see also Maruna et al., 2006). And telling the right story becomes that much more critical when you are disenfranchised and entangled in the legal system or are in need of access to supports, such as shelter or food (Sweet, 2021). A story about structural oppression is unlikely to get you out of prison, even if the story is true.

In contrast, perpetrators in positions of privilege by virtue of their social class, for example, are viewed more favorably than perpetrators in lesser positions of structural privilege (Knight, Giuliano, & Sanchez-Ross, 2001; Pica, Sheahan, & Pozzulo, 2020) and are, of course, less likely to be legally sanctioned (e.g., Miller, 2016). Sometimes it is the case that they don't even need a good story about their transgression, at least in terms of the legal system, because they are viewed so favorably from the start, with the assumption of a good self in need of no repair, or change. Kids who come from "good families," who are viewed as "good boys," are let off easy by judges, who cite wanting to protect their futures (Ferré-Sadurní, 2019). Or cases in which kids are not sanctioned *because* of their privilege, such as the case in "affluenza," where perpetrators are viewed as having a "disease" of privilege that leaves them lacking in motivation, socially isolated, and unable to tell right from wrong, which has been used as a legal excuse for transgressions (Leighton, 2016).

But what a story perpetrators of privilege could tell. Perpetrators, like Harvey Weinstein, exploit their power, their status, their influence, and the vulnerability of women with whom they work. Their stories could *reveal* these aspects of systems that allow such transgressions to occur, even facilitate their occurrence, allowing people like Weinstein to offend for 40 years, while the many who knew what he was up to turned a blind eye.

In fact, it is hard to think of good *public* stories of such atonement for interpersonal violence. This may be due in part to legal concerns with admitting guilt. But those who have been quite credibly accused of such behavior have not *needed* to tell such a story of remorse to curry enough favor to be appointed to the Supreme Court (Brent Kavanaugh and Clarence Thomas), elected president (Donald Trump and Bill Clinton), or to continue or return to celebrity status (Kobe Bryant, Ben Roethlisberger, OJ Simpson). And, of course, there are some well-known perpetrators who *have* been sanctioned, such as Weinstein. But it should be noted that the case of Weinstein included many accusations, unprecedented media attention that centered victims' stories (e.g., Farrow, 2019; Kantor

& Twohey, 2019), and high-profile victims who, in some cases, had access to broad storytelling platforms. This is not to diminish the victims' stories in this case, but to highlight the kind of effort that might be needed for perpetrators to be held to account. But the point here is that true atonement, and change, may not be needed for those in positions of power.

So the story from the perpetrator and society side of things is that there is unlikely to be full engagement in the transgression in ways that induce identity change. Yet even when there is full engagement, there is an expected story template that may be confining even as it may facilitate reentry into society. And that confining story, disproportionately thrust on those who are disenfranchised, is, by definition, focused on the individual and not the system.

But, again, in cases of transgressions there are always at least two parties—perpetrator and victim—and the narrative opportunities and barriers are quite distinct for each party.

THE ETHICS OF CHANGE: COMPARING VICTIM AND PERPETRATOR STORIES

The ways in which victim and perpetrator stories intersect is a meaningful locus of investigation (Pasupathi et al., 2015; Pasupathi, Fivush, & Hernandez-Martinez, 2016; see also Haaken, 2010). Much of this research has examined differences in the narrative features in the stories of victims and perpetrators. Overall, these data suggest that transgression stories seem to be far less about individual differences in storytelling and much more about the role one has played in the event. That is, the nature of the event creates a script that entails different pathways and opportunities for storying transgressions depending on one's role.

One important difference between victim and perpetrator stories has to do with the potential for moral agency available to each party (Pasupathi & Wainryb, 2010). Moral agency is defined as narrating an event by showing that one understands one's own actions, that those actions come from beliefs and desires, and that past actions do not necessarily dictate the present and future. Moral agency focuses on individual responsibility, which resonates with mainstream American culture. And moral agency is more available to perpetrators than victims.

For victims, the story is in some ways defined by passivity—something was done *to* the person. There is far less room for agency in their stories. However, this does not mean that there is no "story work" for victims. They do engage in the labor of trying to understand what happened, perhaps especially because of the widespread denial and invalidation of their stories. This is where self-blame can come in—why *did I go on a date with that guy, walk down that dark street, have another beer.*[2] These explanations serve to fault the victim, a story that is neither healthy nor productive.

In the data comparing perpetrator and victim stories, we see that victims' stories are more likely to be filled with damage, more self-focused, and less growth-oriented, as well as less likely to have happy endings than perpetrators' stories (Pasupathi et al., 2015; see also Baumeister et al., 1990; Lilgendahl et al., 2013; Mansfield, McLean, & Lilgendahl, 2010). When we see growth, it is more likely to be seen in perpetrators' stories. By now we know that a perpetrator's story of growth is more likely to be heard, liked, and validated compared to a victim's story of damage. And the perpetrator's story of growth is potentially a story of change. But where is the change for the victim?

Although victims' stories are less likely to be positive, you might be thinking that if only they *could* tell a "positive" story of change, it would be useful for them as well. Perhaps they could tell a story with agency, with resolution, with meaning about how they have moved through and past this event and come out the other side a new person, a stronger person. Perhaps they could tell a redemptive story about the change in moving from a victim to a survivor (see Delker, Salton, & McLean, 2020). But it might not be that simple. Because isn't that also a confining narrative?

---

2. When asked to report a transgression experience, I have even had participants report *being* assaulted as their *own* transgression—meaning they feel that the assault was their fault (McLean, unpublished data). And we do not see this same kind of blaming behavior with other kinds of crimes, such as with victims of burglary or carjacking, for example, crimes for which there is not an inherent power imbalance (Delker, 2021).

In fact, in her book, *The Politics of Surviving*, Paige Sweet (2021) argues that there is a culturally expected narrative about the journey from being a victim to becoming a survivor. Derived from her interviews with women who have experienced domestic violence, Sweet describes a narrative that comes with its own vocabulary, informed by the medicalized nature of experiencing domestic violence (e.g., diagnoses of posttraumatic stress disorder [PTSD]), and as well as the language of trauma-informed care (e.g., victim). These labels are often coupled with a press for intervention to fix the damaged person, to move the person's identity from victim to survivor, a pressure "to become 'survivors' in order to be seen as responsible and worthy" (p. 3). This intervention is even supposed to come, to be narrated as occurring, in a "revelatory" moment during therapy (pp. 3–4). Sweet argues that although well-intentioned, such a prescribed narrative—with vocabulary and expected events—is severely limiting and potentially damaging. The women with whom Sweet worked saw the identity label of "survivor" as a

> *natural state of being*, the right way to be a respectable woman who deserves care. Attending therapy and becoming a survivor operate as a shorthand for worthiness. Surviving violence requires that women make medicalized claims for personhood and state recognition based on experiences of psychological trauma, a process I refer to—following anthropologists Vinh-Kim Nguyen and Erica Caple James—as *traumatic citizenship*. (p. 5; author's emphasis in italics)

Here again, like the perpetrators, we see this requirement of some form of redemption to enter into a group, to be accepted and validated, to earn (or renew) citizenship.

But this redemptive narrative that we expect from survivors may not be as well received as we think. My colleagues and I have seen that such a redemptive narrative, while certainly liked more than a negative story, is not exactly given full validation. In a series of recent studies, we have seen that—across a range of types of trauma—redemptive stories are preferred to stories that end negatively, not surprisingly (McLean et al., 2020).

But for stories about survivors of interpersonal violence, those redeemed traumas are liked less than redeemed stories about other types of traumas, such as surviving a hurricane or cancer (Delker, Salton, McLean, & Syed, 2020). For victims of interpersonal violence, although we expect—even push for—redemption, telling such a story is no guarantee of acceptance (or healing).

So although there is some wiggle room for a victim to tell a story that *may* get more acceptance, victims are still in a tough spot: Their experiences are less likely to be validated. And that thin validation only comes *if* they tell a story of redemption—a story that may not be true to them.

Such denial serves several purposes. Not hearing the victim's story allows us to deny the systems that allow for such perpetration. If we truly heard what happens to victims (see Miller, 2019), we would see systemic denial in full relief—from the way such incidents are received when reported (if reported at all), to how they are or are not investigated, to how they are treated in court (in the rare case that they get there). We would have to hear the ways in which some victims, by virtue of their class, gender identity, sexual identity, and racial-ethnic identity, experience the system in dramatically different ways. In fact, we "see" interpersonal violence more often, whether it's the perpetrator or the victim, in those who are in lesser positions of power—because those are the people who are arrested, who have fewer resources for legal aid, or who need to engage the system for food and shelter. Those in more privileged positions, who have the resources to keep from getting entangled in these systems, can keep their experiences of violence behind closed doors. This allows us to think that violence does not happen to "good" people or to "respectable" people (see also Gill & Orgad, 2018); in other words, it does not happen to rich white people.

Denying the reality of the victim also allows us to not see ourselves in the victim's story. Dis-identifying with the victim keeps us from seeing the violence around us or from admitting to the violence that we may have experienced (Haaken, 2010; see also Singer, 1997). This depersonalization also keeps us relatively unmotivated to engage in efforts toward structural change, efforts that would take a lot of work.

Finally, as discussed earlier, when perpetrators take responsibility, we can assume they have changed, and their redemption absolves us from thinking about the systems. So the current system that allows a perpetrator to tell a valued redemptive story, while denying the reality of the victim, maintains the status quo.

CONCLUSIONS

In her stunning book, *Hard Knocks: Domestic Violence and the Psychology of Storytelling*, Janice Hakken (2010) argues that one of the major problems with the storying of transgressions about domestic violence is that we assume there is a perpetrator and a victim, setting up a two-sided, binary story that focuses on the basic story line of cause and effect—perpetrator harms victim. Such an unnuanced story allows the denial of a major third character—the system—leaving the story as a "private" matter, left behind closed doors. When listening to advocates from historically and currently marginalized groups, Haaken hears that such simplistic stories perpetuate an individualistic psychology that ignores the cultural and structural problem of violence. And these simplistic stories have been championed by those in positions of privilege and power, including those who control access to resources for victims (Sweet, 2021).

These stories not only passively constrain possibilities for cultural change, but they may also actively work to keep things the same. And they may also create enough constriction that they hamper the potential for authentic personal change. It is only when we recognize this third character and integrate it into our stories that the possibility for addressing structural change can become possible. And it is only then that individuals will have more room and space to tell stories that reflect their experiences and their frameworks of meaning.

But, of course, this kind of storytelling, like any storytelling, is not a solo endeavor. Maruna and Ramsden (2004) argue that successful narrative reconstruction after a transgression is likely to happen in "settings in which individuals feel part of a community (sometimes referred to as

Transgressions as an Opportunity for Change?

a brotherhood or sisterhood) that transcends the present. In this process of historical connectedness, the individual is able to 'seek strength from the experience of those who came before' and is challenged 'to share the strength with those who will follow' (White, 1996, p. 295)" (Maruna & Ramsden, 2004, p. 41). Perhaps the storying of transgressions in a way that privileges historical connectedness and the recognition of the systems and structures at play will lead to a kind of storytelling that aids the collective.

7

The Agency in Resistance

I have spent much of this book talking about the constraints of master narratives, the heavy cultural press for narratives of redemption and growth, the belief that we have more agency to author our own stories than we actually have, and how master narratives and the overemphasis on personal agency serve to maintain inequitable systems of power, such as patriarchy and white supremacy. Because of all this, change is hard to come by—both for the individual and for society.

But now I'd like to flip the script and introduce what might seem like a paradox to my argument. Because there actually *is* a place where we can see a powerful kind of agency revealed in people's stories, an agency that can be used to change and replace harmful and oppressive master narratives. This kind of agentic story, however, does not typically come from those in power. It comes instead from those who *resist* master narratives, those who are often in positions of less structural power.

There is an irony here. People in dominant positions, who believe so mightily in the power of agency—both their own and everyone else's—are usually just passively, some might even say *lazily*, accepting and reinforcing master narratives about people being solely responsible for their life's trajectory. Those in power are likely to think the same level of agency is available to everyone, and that perhaps they are just personally better at exercising their agency on the path to success. In doing so, they reveal how blind they are to the ways they have been supported by the system, a system *designed* to support them (Chapter 3). As Ann Richards once quipped about George Bush Sr.: "He was born on third base and thinks he hit a triple."

> People with social privilege often deny that they enjoy unearned advantages at the expense of others and maintain that they are truly more intelligent, hard-working, determined, etc. than the groups they dominate. It is probably fair to describe the identity dilemma as feeding into the belief that success is about meritocracy (i.e., that effort expended explains individuals rise in the social hierarchy). (Spencer, 2017, p. 295)

Those in power weaponize (often unintentionally) the idea of agency—of individual responsibility and control to effect one's life course—to maintain inequitable systems that support those at the top. Meanwhile, it's those on the margins who must dig much deeper to actually call upon their agency to resist, to truly put their agency to work. So those in power are correct in a way. People do have agency. They just aren't using enough of theirs.

For example, there is an agentic and redemptive story I could tell about how hard I worked in college to get into graduate school. It is a story of late-night studying, long hours in the library, the writing and rewriting (and rewriting) of papers, a story of commuting around the Bay Area to various volunteer research assistant positions—interviewing caregivers for a study on attachment, slicing mouse brains, organizing data for studies on adolescent psychopathology—all with the crowning achievement of acceptance into a PhD program. This is a story about my personal and agentic efforts—my hard work—leading to success. It is a story that fits a template we know well. And although it is not an untrue story, it is also not a full story.

It is *not* a story about receiving a Pell Grant and low-interest student loans for tuition and expenses, or having enough family support to own a reliable car that allowed me to commute to a school across (government built and maintained) bridges and freeways, or about the personal ties that helped me to get the research positions that were so important to my graduate school applications. It is also not a story about the education my parents (and grandparents) received, where I was born, the good schools I went to, familial connections for jobs, or the way teachers and employers responded to me by virtue of the color of my white skin.

For those in power, telling only the cherry-picked story about hard work and success is undeniably part of the process of unconsciously maintaining the status quo. It takes an effortful step, reflective work, to see—to admit—that such success is derived from systems as well, to see that our success is not only about our own efforts, our own agency. If our own personal success stories serve to maintain systems that are inequitable and oppressive, and if we *think* we have agency in how we tell our stories, some of us might want to reflect on our complicity in that maintenance.

But back to flipping the script.

RESISTANCE AS A PARTICULAR KIND OF AGENCY

In this chapter, I use the term "resistance narratives"[1] to illustrate a particular kind of agency. I have previously used the term "alternative narratives" to label narratives told by those who do not align with master narratives. However, alternative narratives are not necessarily meant to disrupt or dismantle master narratives. They *may*, but they may also exist alongside master narratives, primarily known and used by those who find their lives represented in these alternative templates. Alternative narratives become resistance narratives when they actively and intentionally challenge master narratives: resistance narratives don't "*reflect* a shift in understanding. They set out to *cause* a shift" (Nelson, 2001, p. 156). That means that resistance narratives are not necessarily about changing one's own identity (though they can be). They are about changing the systems that validate certain identities, while denying others.

Rogers and Way (2018) argue that developmental science has traditionally overlooked the process of resistance in its focus on the classic Piagetian

---

1. Sometimes called counternarratives (Andrews, 2002; Nelson, 2001; Rogers et al., 2020).

concepts applied to processes of learning: assimilation and accommodation. In understanding how social ideologies develop, in particular, these processes do not account for acts of resistance to social hierarchies and oppression. Assimilating to the status quo, or accommodating one's templates to new information, are processes focused solely on the individual. Without space for resistance, "[f]raming human development this way means that growing up is, in essence, a natural process of reproducing societal inequalities" (Rogers & Way, 2018, p. 7).

But luckily, resistance has been studied extensively in other disciplines such as philosophy, critical race theory, feminist studies, criminal justice, and education, to name a few (e.g., Crossing et al., 2022; Delgado & Stefancic, 2001; Gilligan, 2011; hooks, 1990; Moton & Blount-Hill, 2022; Nelson, 2001; Solórzano & Yosso, 2002; Tuck & Yang, 2014). Scholars in these disciplines show that the agency called upon in telling resistance stories can be used to disrupt and dismantle master narratives. They also emphasize the *collective* work of resistance, the necessity of connecting to and working with other people. Resistance is not a job for the solo storyteller. Rogers and Way (2021) call "resistance for liberation" a "collective uplift" (p. 4) (see also Bañales & Rivas-Drake, 2022).

RESISTANCE AS A DEVELOPMENTAL PROCESS

Nelson (2001, p. 169) identifies three stages in the process of disrupting, displacing, and replacing master narratives. The first is a more internal step of a person *refusing* a master narrative by denying that it applies to one's own experiences, beginning personal work on a resistance story. The second is the interpersonal *repudiation* of a master narrative by using one's developing resistance story to oppose others who are imposing a master narrative on the self. The third is the *contesting* of a master narrative by systematically publicizing one's resistance story.

Similarly, Fish and Counts (2021) argue that resistance stories can be cultivated as people learn, and are given space, to tell stories that are true to their own experiences, rather than the stereotyped tales with which they are confronted. As these personal stories develop, individuals can connect with others to begin the process of building a collective story. As these personal and collective stories that resist master narratives become visible, they trouble the waters, beginning to disrupt and change the status quo.

Finally, Rogers and Way (2021) define resistance as "the ways humans consciously and unconsciously reject or counter dehumanizing ideologies and question social hierarchies" (p. 3). They go on to argue that resistance is a natural, and necessary, component of human development:

> Resistance to harmful ideologies that undermine such core human needs is not simply a developmental competency but an engine of healthy development, a human capacity driven by our need to stay connected to our humanity and the humanity of others. (p. 3)

This is an important point: Resistance is not only about changing oppressive systems; it is also a natural part of human development and activity, something *all of us* can do. Much of the scholarship on resistance has been done with those who are marginalized, but I will return to the role of resistance for those in power at the close of this chapter.

Despite the natural ability to resist, it is hard work. It is tiring. It is burdensome. Rogers and Way (2021) argue that it must be "nurtured." Luckily there are scholars developing a knowledge base about how to nurture that work.

INTERPERSONAL CONTEXTS FOR RESISTANCE STORIES

Jill Fish provides a compelling example of how to nurture stories of resistance, a project that she calls "emancipatory" (see Fish & Counts, 2021, for a review of work in this area). Her work involves the intentional challenge to master narratives about Native Americans found in mainstream culture, stories represented in movies, TV shows, books, sports mascots, and advertising campaigns. These stories and images that depict Native Americans as poor, as drunk, as either aggressive or simple-minded, contain damaging stereotypes that are especially harmful given the invisibility of Native Americans in dominant white culture (e.g., Fryberg, Markus, Oyserman, & Stone, 2008; Fryberg & Townsend, 2008; see also Syed, Santos, Yoo, & Juang, 2018).

Beyond their untruths, these false stories also leave little space for stories that need hearing, such as the history of colonization and genocide, the stealing of land, and the forced residential boarding schools that ripped families apart. These false stories also leave little space for stories of strength in the face of atrocity, stories about how culture was preserved and passed on from generation to generation, stories about the passing on of wisdom, of language, of song and ceremony, stories about the power of survival and resilience, or what Gerald Vizenor (2008) calls *survivance*.

These false stories are also decidedly *not* about self-determination (Fish & Counts, 2021).[2] In listening to the stories that are actually told by Indigenous people, Fish argues that we can see how "historically- and culturally-salient stories can empower and liberate Native peoples to live more self-determined futures, and full and authentic lives" (p. 240). Fish and Counts argue that storytelling "is ideal for shifting master narratives because it recognizes the will and determination of Native peoples as active co-constructors of their lived experiences" (p. 244).

Fish and Counts (2021) nurture such stories through the creation of a space (physical and psychological) that facilitates individuals' construction of their stories through the written word, pictures, music, and video.

OrigiNatives is a digital storytelling project that travels to host workshops for Native American and Indigenous peoples to create original digital stories about our cultures, histories, and lives. By combining storytelling with digital media technologies, OrigiNatives places the power to change harmful colonial narratives about what it

---

2. Self-determination is not only a policy, passed in 1975 to bring autonomy to educational practices for Native Americans (Indian Self Determination and Education Assistance Act; see Deyhle & Swisher, 1997), and a right recognized by the United Nations for sovereign governing; it is also a movement to combat the historical and ongoing violence of colonization.

means to be Native American in the hands of Native American and Indigenous peoples themselves. The digital stories created as a part of OrigiNatives give voice to how Indigenous peoples leverage land-based, ancestral, oral, and intergenerational wisdom to determine our pasts, presents, and futures beyond the confines of colonialism. (https://www.jillianfish.com/originatives)

As individuals tell their stories, the process becomes collective, revealing the power of gathering and accumulating stories that challenge the dominant discourse. Fish and Counts argue that such stories are

> first and foremost a community project, that is for and by the people; simultaneously healing and liberating Native peoples from the legacy of colonialism. Centering culture and community enabled participants to fully engage, reflect on, and question the stories that constituted their sense of selves, empowering them to give voice to experiences often deemed illegitimate or invisible in Western society. (p. 262)

In the words of some of the some of those who participated in the project of sharing their stories (https://www.jillianfish.com/originatives):

Joe (2018) of the Red Lake Band of Ojibwe recalled: *When I moved from the rez to the city, I think I finally really started to think from an outside perspective about my culture, where I come from, who I am, and what matters to me. So much has been lost in Native culture that we are now working to revitalize, but one of the big things I personally believe in is that my culture is not static and has always existed and continued to grow despite what was taken from us.*

Shirley (2018) of the Red Lake Band of Ojibwe recalled: *I firmly believe I am here for a reason—that Gitchi manitou sent me here to help Native people in whatever way I can. My vision for my Anishinabe people is to help them become healthy and happy people again, the way we were a long time ago. I would like us to go back to our original values and teachings of sharing, caring, humility, bravery, honesty and courage. We are a fantastic and beautiful people and are not just what the media portrays us as.*

Millie (2018) of the White Earth Band of Ojibwe recalled: *Journaling, youth work, and service to my community, have been a major piece of my healing. More importantly, they have all served as a means to discovering what my cultural identity means to me. I'm Native. I'm proud. I'm forgiving. I'm evolving. I'll live the rest of my years being a servant to others outside of myself . . . my family, my community, and the unknown. To me, that's what it means to be Native.*

From Joe, Shirley, and Millie we hear stories that challenge the invisibility of Native Americans, testifying to their very *existence* through time, stories that defy the expectations, tropes, and stereotypes of our society, stories that are collective, shared, and powerful.

In a similar project, Indigenous researchers at a nonprofit organization called Children of the Setting Sun Productions are working to gather and uplift voices of the Salmon People, members of Coast Salish tribes and nations along the west coast of what is now called North America. Their work is focused specifically on the dramatic decline of salmon, and using the stories they have gathered about the importance of salmon to their livelihoods, to the natural ecology of the region, and to their identities to make structural and systemic change. Their goal is not small: They are doing powerful, agentic work to combat climate change, work that is, by definition, collective, and that has the survival and the thriving of future generations at heart.

The Children of the Setting Sun Productions (CSSP) is embarking on a journey to tell the story of the ancient bond between the Native people and salmon. Through storytelling, we will speak to the core issues at the heart of salmon decline: a disconnect, and therefore a disrespect for Mother Earth, fellow human beings, and ourselves. We will build awareness of how this disconnect has led to broken treaty promises and a devastating loss to Native Americans.

The Salmon People Project will make it clear the Coast Salish Tribes will forever fight for nothing less than the abundant return of salmon in their natural habitat and the complete restoration of the Salish Sea. (https://settingsunproductions.org)

Like Fish's project, this work is "nurtured" through ceremony, connection, and the creation of space for the intimacies of storytelling. Research interviews are often done in participants' homes, with family present. The process begins with the sharing of food, and introductions for everyone involved—participants and researchers—sharing who their families are, how they identify themselves, and what brings them to this work of healing the earth. And like Fish's work, this project is focused on the power of stories to sustain and strengthen individuals and communities, to displace the colonists' mainstream stories with the experience and knowledge of the Coast Salish peoples, and to demonstrate their power and sovereignty.

One of the markers of the work just described is the need to intentionally create space and time for the gathering, developing, and sharing of stories. This is part of the nurturing of resistance stories that are so emotional and labor-intensive to tell. These spaces are also particularly important when groups have differential or unequal access to stories about their group. For example, both Children of the Setting Sun Productions and Jill Fish and her team have created public platforms for stories, in part so that those who have not had access to these stories within their own homes or communities can engage with them.

In my work with Nic Weststrate, we share the concern with these other research teams about the kinds of stories that marginalized people have access to—in our case, within the LGBTQ+ community. LGBTQ+ youth are often raised in families and communities who do not share their sexual or gender identities (Turner et al., under review). As with other groups placed on the margins of a society, members of the LGBTQ+ community are exposed to, and sometimes internalize, harmful stories about their group, making critical the need for strong stories to counteract and replace harmful stories (Turner et al., in preparation). For example, we heard from youth about what it would be like to have queer elders who could play a role in passing on such stories:

> If I were to have that [contact] I feel like it would impact me tremendously. Being able to share that part of me and learn new things with someone who knows what I am feeling would be a special moment for me. I would specifically like to learn about any cultural practices in my community as I find those interesting.
>
> I would like to hear about a personal experience from an elder. There are many experiences I have that I do not share with anyone I know and I would like to know that I am not alone in these experiences. I would specifically want to learn about how someone else had adjusted to discovering their identity late in life and dealt with their fears they had around their identity. I would like to feel less alone in my experience dealing with these issues.

The desire for cultural and interpersonal connection and belonging is strong and, I would argue, necessary for the cultivation of resistance stories. Nic and I are drawing from the wisdom of these other research teams, believing it is possible that the creation of space, ceremony, and connection will nurture the sharing of stories across generations of LGBTQ+ people, thus cultivating strength and resilience, and leading to the replacement of harmful master narratives.

Nic has called stories that are intergenerationally transmitted within marginalized communities a "developmental resource" (Weststrate et al., 2023), making access to them an issue of equity. Indeed, access to such stories works to ameliorate what philosopher Miranda Fricker (2007) calls *epistemic injustice*, which has two forms (see also Tsosie, 2012). *Hermeneutical* injustice occurs when those who are in the stage of learning are denied access to knowledge and meaning-making frameworks that are necessary to understand their identities and navigate their marginality, which is reflected in the quotes earlier from those without access to queer elders. Collecting stories and making them available to others, or creating spaces for sharing stories, provides access to the knowledge needed for identity work and for resistance to be nurtured. *Testimonial injustice* occurs when people are not heard, when they are discounted as knowers. When these resistance stories are given space to be shared, the knowers become heard.

In short, the work of resistance takes psychological and even physical space. It takes ceremony and connection. It is no easy task to understand one's identity as embedded within systems of power, privilege, and oppression that need resisting. And community strength, connection, and collaboration are essential ingredients (see also French et al., 2020: Syed & McLean, 2022a). The agency here is collective.

SOCIOPOLITICAL CONTEXTS OF RESISTANCE STORIES

The research described earlier points to the need for the ongoing cultivation of stories of resistance to dismantle oppressive systems, and for that work to be done in connection with others. There are also particular moments in time when opportunities to cultivate the agency to resist increase.

One especially impactful study highlighted the role that living history and current events might have on compelling youth to embark on the path toward resistance. Rogers, Rosario, Padilla, and Foo (2021) followed kids in middle childhood who were interviewed about their racial identity in 2014 and again in 2016, a period that covered Michael Brown's murder in Ferguson, Missouri, and the increasing presence and awareness of the Black Lives Matter (BLM) movement. Rogers and her team predicted that widespread cultural events would impact developing identities, and that the position of the person in the system would matter. Or, put differently, it is not possible to understand identity development *without* attending to the meaning of these events for people at different positions within a racialized hierarchy.

Their first finding was that the importance of the children's racial identities increased over these 2 years. But this increase was not due to simple maturation; the researchers saw no age-related change in racial identity importance. And the researchers saw this change primarily for the Black and multiracial children, not the white children (see also Umaña-Taylor et al., 2014). So the change in ratings was tied to the sociopolitical context of their developing racial identities—the events that occurred between 2014 and 2016—*and* to their position in the racial hierarchy. These results challenge traditional developmental theories that rely on age-based maturation and are decontextualized from the actual contexts of development (see also McLean & Riggs, 2022). It is simply not possible to understand racial identity development decontextualized from this system, for anyone. Because, of course, the *lack* of development for the white children is a finding as well, showing that their identity development (or lack thereof) is also tied to the system and their position in it. *All* children are living in a racialized system, and *all* of their developmental trajectories are embedded within it (Crossing et al., 2022; Moffitt, Rogers, & Dastrup, 2021; Rogers et al., 2021; Rogers, 2022).

Rogers and her team also found that the children's understanding of race as *structural* increased over time (this is compared to understanding race as personal, such as about skin color), and this was the case across kids with different racial identities. Structural concerns included discussion of police brutality, historic and current injustices, and the BLM movement specifically. That is, the kids came to understand how their racial identities were tied to the sociopolitical context. The authors provided the following interview excerpt from a boy they call Steven, who increased on such structural reasoning over the time of the study. The excerpt is from the second assessment, in 2016:

Q: What does it mean to be Black?
A: Um well, it's hard because it's the cops that are killing us for stupid stuff. So like, if you think like the people that are supposed to help you are killing you, then imagine life in five more years; it's gonna be like your friends are killing you and then everybody is killing you. That's what I feel like. So, if the cops are already killing us for doing nothin', then you might as well just step out the door and get shot.
Q: How do you think things would be different if you weren't Black?
A: I would get all the stuff and nobody will look at me like I was a target.

Steven's understanding of his race is tied to the moment—to the racialized violence in the country that make him feel like a target. Interestingly, in 2014, two years before this interview, Steven's ideas about race were also tied to the moment. He thought that there was "nothing" hard about being Black, and that there had been a lot of change for the better in terms of race relations over time. When asked why things had changed, he said, "Cause Obama became the president. Our first Black president."

Racial identity is never developing in a vacuum, and sociopolitical events provide opportunities, sometimes tragic ones, to understand how one's own identity is part of the systems and structures of society. And these opportunities can help us to understand what needs resisting. But it is likely that Steven did not come to this new understanding of race as structurally embedded entirely on his own.

THE INTERTWINING OF THE PERSONAL, INTERPERSONAL, AND SOCIOPOLITICAL CONTEXTS

To be clear, it is not simply that events "happen" and identities develop. There is true labor to making meaning of these events, and not everyone does it. In the case of Rogers et al.'s study, the white youth, who were in the same sociopolitical context—in the same school—did not experience the same change and development in their racial identities as the Black and multiracial kids.

And when the labor of storytelling happens, it is best facilitated by the coalescing of personal, interpersonal, and contextual alignment. Because research on resistance stories makes clear that the agency to resist is not only a personal or interpersonal act. And it is not only the result of sociopolitical events and social movements that inspire change. It is all of these things together.

In the case of racialized violence, we see how creating a connection between the personal, interpersonal, and sociopolitical contexts is a necessary ingredient for resistance. For example, Anderson, O'Brien, Caughy, and Owen (2021) provide a compelling account of the strategies that Black parents use when having "The Talk" about what to do when encountering police with their 10- to 11-year-old children. Given that encounters with the police are disproportionality likely to occur, and to end in harm, for Black people compared to white people (e.g., GBD Police Violence US Subnational Collaborators, 2021), for many parents the primary goal of these conversations is safety: talking to children about how to behave to survive. But for some parents, there is a twin, and sometimes, competing message of what Rogers and Way (2018) call "resistance for liberation." In Anderson et al.'s study, such resistance manifested in discussions about understanding the systemic bias in policing, the importance of naming that bias and holding law enforcement to account, and the ability to resist and fight against injustice. Of course, such resistance may come at the cost of safety, an agonizing dilemma for parents and their children. But we do see a pathway toward resistance here—in the coinciding of widespread major events along with the interpersonal space for discussion of those events, so that children like Steven begin to see their identities as a part of the sociopolitical context (see also, e.g., Hughes et al., 2006; Jones & Neblett, 2016, 2019; Stevenson & Arrington, 2009).

The final implication of this research—and a message directed most specifically to those of us who are scientists—is that when we center context, structure, and systems, when we integrate them into our study designs, when we *measure* them, we see that they matter (Fish & Syed, 2018; French et al., 2020; Helms, 1993; Moffitt & Rogers, 2022; Rogers, Niwa, Chung, Yip, & Chae, 2021; Rogers, 2022; Rogers et al., 2023). The personal story and the structural story are *both* important. They are *both* true. They cannot be separated. Our frame needs to shift not from individual *to* structure, but to individual *and* structure (Rogers et al., 2021; see also Moffitt et al., 2021). When we as researchers do *not* attend to structure and systems in our research questions and study designs, our science will remain sorely compromised in our ability to understand human functioning and development, and we do a disservice, a disrespect, to our participants and to their stories.

The Need for a Different Story

In her Ted Talk about "The Danger of a Single Story," the writer Chimamanda Ngozi Adichie (2009) argues that a hallmark of an oppressive master narrative—of a single story—is that "[i]t robs people of dignity." Hegemonic master narratives work to undermine the strength, and even existence, of groups who have been marginalized by dominant people and systems of power, people and systems that relentlessly try to define oppressed and marginalized groups only by their deficits. That deficit story becomes the prevailing story about oppressed groups, the story given the most airtime, the most power, leaving the impression that it is the only story. Adichie argues that the course of the story, and its meaning, is defined by where it begins. To counteract that single story, we need to start *in a different place*.

> Start the story with the arrows of the Native Americans, and not with the arrival of the British, and you have an entirely different story. Start the story with the failure of the African state, and not with the colonial creation of the African state, and you have an entirely different story. (Adichie, 2009)

The scholars whose work I have reviewed in this chapter all started their research in a different place. In all cases they integrated history, culture, structures, and systems. They started their stories earlier, and in doing so provided a fuller picture. They also brought the full weight of the strength of the communities with whom they were working. In fact, when researchers take the full context and history of oppression into account, it would be hard to ignore the strength that community members have shown to survive, and even to thrive. Doing work on resistance means recognizing those who have been oppressed are not passive victims, but that they have strength and power, that they have agency, that they are fully human.

BROADENING THE RESPONSIBILITY FOR RESISTANCE

But as Rogers and Way (2021) argue, "[t]he *ability* to respond does not and should not equate to *liability* for the oppressions that necessitate such responses" (p. 5). They continue:

> As a field, this focus on resistance directs our attention away from "fixing" individuals and families and toward disrupting the cultural ideologies that dehumanize and lead to the necessity to foster resistance for liberation. *It is imperative that the study of resistance not become another individual-focused approach* but a call to acknowledge the cultural ideological context and the natural human agency to disrupt it. (p. 6, emphasis in italics)

And following this argument, the responsibility for resistance does not fall only on the oppressed. Recall that Rogers and Way (2021) argued strongly that resistance is a human capacity. Which means that those in power can also resist the system. And although there is less risk to the powerful than for those who are *already in* vulnerable structural positions, there is *some* risk. There is much uncomfortable personal work to be done in order to undo the stories that have been cemented, to undo those stories that provide privilege and cover to those who tell them (e.g., Tatum, 2000). As Margaret Beale Spencer argues, those in power have done some serious mental contortions to justify their identities, contortions that need to be undone by developing an awareness of the reality that they have distorted:

> to avoid the dissonance and confusion that result from being confronted with one's own privilege, individuals must uphold a distorted/inflated view of their own innate value and justify their oppression (either overt and hostile or subtle and indirect) of others . . . to

become aware of one's privilege is to accept one's responsibility to surrender unfair advantages and entitlements, recognize one's role in the system that reinforces injustices—a feat that proves challenging for some people. (Spencer, 2017, p. 295)

Doing this kind of work means seeing that it is not only the oppressed, those on the margins, who have been impacted by the system. Everyone is impacted by the system. One of the reasons the white children did *not* show growth in their racial identity development from 2014 to 2016 (Rogers et al., 2021)—why they remained *stable* in their identities, why they did not change—is because they are impacted by the system that makes their racial identity the norm, and thus, comfortably invisible (Moffitt & Rogers, 2022; Moffitt et al., 2021).

In terms of the privilege of race, there is a model for white racial identity development, pioneered by Janet Helms (e.g., 1990), in which people pass through stages, sometimes cyclically, of learning about their racial identity and their privileged position (see also Moffitt & Rogers, 2022). Interestingly, the last stage is called "autonomy," in which one has both a positive view of one's own racial identity *and is actively engaged* in the pursuit of social justice, or resistance. Spencer (2017) argues that active reflection and self-examination "ultimately encourages greater acceptance of responsibility for individual and systems change associated with the unfair accrual of significant benefits" (p. 296).

Moffitt et al. (2021) argue that in developing their racial identity, to understand their position in the hierarchy, white people also need to make meaning of their experiences, often in interpersonal contexts, and in light of sociopolitical events (see also Moffitt & Rogers, 2022). For example, although most white parents do not discuss race with their children, or they socialize a color-blind ideology (Abaied & Perry, 2021; Chae, Rogers, & Yip, 2020; Perry, Skinner, & Abaied, 2019), both deeply problematic for the development of resistance, white parents *can* engage in a form of resistance in another form of "The Talk." There are certainly many current events that provide opportunities to do so. Moffitt and Rogers (2022) argue that parents, and other socializing agents, must name the developmental context of white supremacy for children to understand the system in which they are developing, the system from which they derive privilege, and the system for which they share responsibility to either maintain or resist (see also Loyd & Gaither, 2018; Moffitt & Rogers, 2022; Perry et al., 2021). To not discuss this context and history with white children, or to socialize a colorblind ideology, are acts that serve to maintain systems of racial oppression and privilege (see Hagerman, 2014; Moffitt et al., 2021; Moffitt & Rogers, 2022).

The starting point for this socializing work is to understand that those of us who passively internalize and reify master narratives are engaging in a process that maintains structural inequity and oppression, a process that keeps some of us in our position of privilege and power and others of us on the margins. This goes for those of us who are scientists as well. We can passively internalize master narratives and reify them in the people we study (and don't study), the questions we ask (and don't ask), the concepts we measure (and don't measure), and the interpretations we offer (and don't offer) (Helms, 1993; Moffitt & Rogers, 2022; Rogers et al., 2023; Teo, 2010). Or we can choose to resist.

There is an individual responsibility to understand one's own passivity, to understand that there are *actions* one takes—no less damaging if taken unintentionally—to passively uphold the system, actions one takes to refuse agency, and to hide from collective responsibility. To relinquish agency is a choice, and it is a choice one has the agency to change.

PART IV

Conclusion

8

Our Scientific Responsibility for Change

Since I began doing the scholarly work of studying narrative identity development, some of the most common questions I am asked from academics, students, and laypeople alike include these: What should the narrative intervention be? How do we help people to narrate their experiences in ways that will make them happier and healthier? How do we get them to *change their stories* so that they are happier and healthier? Since those who tell more redemptive stories are happier, shouldn't we help people to craft their tragedies and traumas to match that template?

This intervention question has bugged me since I first heard it. I have just never felt comfortable with this idea of changing people's stories to the "right" one (see Mansfield, Pasupathi, & McLean, 2022). But I was never quite clear why. I would mutter things about not having enough data yet, but my discomfort always seemed murky. I couldn't quite put my finger on it. I *did* know that redemptive stories were *not* always associated with good things, particularly when we worked with youth on the margins (Breen & McLean, 2016; McLean & Mansfield, 2010; McLean, Wood, & Breen, 2013; Sales, Merrill, & Fivush, 2013). But I think the press for liking redemption was so strong, in me, a participant in this culture, that I couldn't quite see the full story. It wasn't until I realized we would be asking people to change their stories to align with a master narrative that I was able to explain my discomfort. And to realize how potentially damaging such a move could be. So my mutterings were right: We *don't* have enough data. We don't have enough data on alternative hypotheses. We don't have enough data from more and different kinds of people. And we don't have enough data that attend to culture, systems, and structures.

And the intervention question is still sidestepping the real problem. Interventions are aimed at the person. Although many of us think a reasonable outcome variable would be subjective well-being, or psychological well-being, that is not getting at the root of the problem. In discussing systems of oppression in psychological science, Rogers and Way (2021) ask: *What does it mean to be adjusted in a maladjusted world*? If we continue to focus on the individual outcome, we will continue to focus on the individual predictor. What would happen if we thought of adjustment and psychological health as collective? What if the intervention was directed at the *culture* to improve the lives of individuals?

There is a broad reckoning in psychology right now over myriad issues: basic scientific practices around openness and replicability (e.g., Syed, 2019, Vazire, 2018; Yarkoni, 2022), diversity and representation in our science (e.g., Arshad & Chung, 2022; Roberts, Bareket-Shavit, Dollins, Goldie, & Mortenson, 2020; Syed & Kathawalla, 2021; Syed, Santos, Yoo, & Juang, 2018), structures of power and gatekeeping that deny access to participation (e.g., Blount-Hill, St. John, Moton, & Ajil, 2022; Lewis, 2021), the necessity of using different and more socially just approaches in our work (e.g., Crossing et al., 2022; Fish, 2021; Gill & Orgad, 2018; Nzinga et al., 2018; Rogers, Moffitt, McLean, & Syed, 2023; Salter & Adams, 2013), and the responsibility we have to communicate our science accurately (see Lewis, 2021; Teo, 2010). This book is a part of that chorus calling for real self-reflection and collective reflection on what we do and how we do it.

My particular call has to do with how our biases have shaped the narrow focus on individual agency in narration, limiting our attention to the role of structures and systems, and how our infatuation with personal growth and redemption has limited our attention to whether and how actual change occurs.

> In a society deeply scarred by inequality and injustice, resources to develop resilience are offered as ways to navigate and survive pain, risk, difficulties, and unhappiness. Yet, in promoting elasticity, affirmation, and inspiration, they remain trapped within an individualistic and psychological framing that we suggest is becoming more and more central to contemporary forms of neoliberal governance, and silences critique of structural inequality. (Gill & Orgad, 2018, p. 491)

PROPOSALS FOR CHANGE IN OUR SCIENTIFIC PRACTICES

A weighty responsibility for change falls on the scientists who are in positions of power. There are plenty of current proposals and arguments to change how we do our science at the level of the individual scholar, as well as the structural and systemic levels (e.g., Ledgerwood et al., 2022; Roberts et al., 2020). Here, I offer four things that I have been asking myself to consider in my own research practices, and that I pose to you, the reader, to also consider.

First, stop and consider whether the phenomenon under study has been fully *described*. Observation and then description are the first stages of experimental design—*before* explanation and prediction (e.g., Bringmann, Elmer, & Eronen, 2022; Rozin, 2001; Scheel, Tiokhin, Isager, & Lakens, 2001; Syed, 2022; Yarkoni & Westfall, 2017). So many of us go to explanation and prediction before we know what we are studying. This is hugely problematic. How can we change something if we don't know what it is? This means potentially throwing out many of our "validated" and "reliable" measures and allowing ourselves, *forcing ourselves*, to start fresh (for similar arguments, see, e.g., Crossing et al., 2020; Settles, Warner, Buchanan, & Jones, 2020). Indeed, questioning where and how our measures and methodologies were developed, and our reliance on positivist and postpositivist paradigms, reveals the biases in how we have developed our toolkit from the very beginning (see also Blount-Hill & Ajil, 2023; Rogers et al., 2023; Syed & McLean, 2022b). We are always limited by the tools we use, and it is time to recognize the limits of those tools, to recognize where they came from, and what values are embedded within them.

Second, in service of better describing the phenomenon, *listen* to stories from more people (e.g., Blount-Hill et al., 2022; Rogers, Moffitt, & Meiling, 2021). Simple. More people. Listen to more people who are different from each other and different from who I usually listen to. I am likely to hear different stories. I am likely to learn something new. I am likely to do better research, because when I listen to more people, I will have a better description of what I am trying to measure. Describing a phenomenon using a very narrow group of people results in a very narrow, and incomplete, description.

Third, *look* for systems and structures when listening to stories. What role do systems and structures play in the stories told? How can I see them in the actual stories? What are the explicit references to systems and structures? How do they support functioning and development, and how do they restrict and oppress functioning and development? Where do these systems and structures seem invisible to the storyteller, and can I vivify them (see Syed & McLean, 2021a, for empirical approaches to this recommendation)?

Finally, who benefits from which stories? For example, when we tell a story of racial disparities, who benefits? Who is that story for? Teo (2010) argues that it is our job to help make meaning of our results, because they are not neutral facts (see also Fox & Fine, 2013; Syed et al., 2018). They are observations that always have a context, and it is our job to provide that context and interpretation. And to recognize and name that they are *interpretations*, which *people* make. People who have particular perspectives that shape the interpretations they make. Our stories always serve a purpose. Ask yourself each time you are writing up your results and discussion: What purpose does this story serve? *Who's* purpose does the story serve?

So what happens when we do these things.? Here are a few examples.

My colleague, Jordan Booker (Booker, Brakke, Sales, & Fivush, 2022), published a recent paper in which he collected narratives about life challenges from Black women college students—a group that is not well represented in the field of narrative identity (stories from *more people*). Booker et al. were interested in how personal growth manifested in the narratives. For those women who reported experiencing personal growth in the narration of their life challenges, the team coded the content of that growth. What were the kinds of things that made the women feel like they had grown? Booker's team documented some themes that were consistent with traditional approaches to growth that might sound familiar, like positive self-acceptance and feelings of agency. But there were also themes that hadn't been captured by prior work, such as the importance of positive group identity and community unity, a theme focused on the collective (see Chapter 7).

Booker's approach nicely captures the importance of listening to more people to create a fuller description of a phenomenon than had been documented in prior, narrower literature. Further, in one of the narratives excerpted in the paper, Booker and colleagues show how the importance of group connection emerged for one woman. She narrated her experiences of the need for group unity arising from the context of going to a predominantly white high school. The segregated educational *system* was clear in her narrative, if one was looking for it.

In another example, Onnie Rogers (Rogers, Versey, & Cielto, 2021) published a recent paper in which she and her team listened to what 93% of Black girls said in interviews about their ethnic-racial and gender identities: that hair is important. The girls viewed hair as a marker of their identities. Hair is not in contemporary theories of identity. In fact, nothing about the body is present in theories of identity development (e.g., Breen, Lewis, & Sutherland, 2013; Pasupathi, 2015). I wonder if that would be the case if people who were developing our foundational theories of identity development were also those placed on the margins by virtue of their skin color, their hair, their gender identity, or their physical ability. What if our participant pools had been larger and more representative when we developed our initial measures? It's hard to imagine transgender researchers and participants not talking about their bodies in relation to their identities (Bradford & Syed, 2019). It's hard to imagine those with physical disabilities not talking about their bodies as relevant to their identities (Adler, 2018; Adler et al., 2022).

But the idea here is not just to run out and grab a bunch of marginalized people and "capture" their stories, for your benefit as a researcher. Doing this kind of work requires an ethic of care, a moral imperative. I always tell my students that stories are "precious." That we need to respect the stories and the storytellers. Often this means practical things, such as not talking about the stories we are working on in lab on the bus with each other because you never know who might hear you. It also means that we discuss our observations of narratives respectfully, even as we might have a hard time reading particular stories or disagree with particular perspectives. It also means considering *how* we ask questions and *who* is asking them.

One of my recent graduate students, Kit Turner, developed a program of research to examine whether LGBTQ+ youth had access to queer elders to help them to learn about the history, practices, and culture of their group—whether and how they experienced socialization about and support for their gender and sexual identities as they were growing up. Part of the project was a large survey-based assessment, and part was a series of intensive one-on-one interviews. Two things struck me. First, in the interviews it was important that the researchers disclose their own investment in the project and how their identities were relevant to the project (see Josselson, 2013; Gilligan, 2015; Rogers, Versey, & Cielto, 2021). The participants needed to know where the researchers were coming from in order to fully consent to sharing their stories. Second, in listening to the interviews, it quickly became clear that the interview itself was an intervention. That asking youth about whether they had learned about the history of the queer community made many realize that they hadn't and that they were missing something really important. These interviews were intensely emotional. After the first one or two, Kit and I spoke about priorities in the interview. Taking a stance of neutrality, "stick to the script," would mean not responding to, or acknowledging, the emotionality and intensity of the interview. But we quickly realized our priority was not scientific neutrality, or the positivist value placed on researcher objectivity. Because there is no neutrality. Validating and supporting these participants as their stories unfolded was the most important part of the process (see also Gilligan, 2105; Josselson, 2013; McClelland, 2017; Rogers & Way, 2018; Rogers, Moffitt, & Jones, 2021). These are people, and they need to be treated as such. If our data are "tainted" by our bias, at least we offered a safe and supportive space for people to explore their identities. That feels immensely more important to me than attempting to create a veil of neutrality.

The second thing that struck me about Kit's project came from the survey data. We had some open-ended prompts about experiences with queer elders. For those who did *not* have queer elders, we asked what it would have meant to them to have such experiences (I excerpted some of those in Chapter 7). The responses were painful and powerful, and deeply enlightening. But the responses didn't really fit with the preregistered plan we had laid out and the specific research questions we had posed for the main project. We had added this question almost as a politeness, so that when people checked "no" to the question about whether they had a queer elder, they had a chance to share their thoughts and experiences with us. So these responses were not going to make it into our initial, planned manuscript. But we decided that they had to go somewhere. It would be disrespectful to these participants to not share their wisdom and desires with the larger public. They took the time to provide such thoughtful answers to our questions, so we needed to take the time to work through them and communicate them. The story is for them as well.

There is an entire methodology of participatory action research (e.g., Cammarota & Fine, 2008; Katsiaficas, 2015; Stoudt, Fox, & Fine, 2012; Weis & Fine, 2012), where researchers partner with participants in developing and executing research. Where participants are valued as "knowers," as experts, on their own experiences, understanding that the researcher is not always the expert. We could all take lessons from this kind of approach. It empowers participants and brings opportunities for new kinds of knowledge to be uncovered. And it is very, very messy. But humans are very, very messy. Understanding our psychologies is a messy, messy endeavor. One perhaps not entirely well-suited to the positivist research paradigms adopted from other scientific disciplines (Rogers et al., 2023; Syed & McLean, 2022b). If we added more tools to our toolkit and valued more variety in how we approach our questions, we might be doing a much better job.

WE ARE ALWAYS BIASED, SO LET'S BE TRANSPARENT ABOUT IT

In arguing for greater transparency about the biases we all have, Rogers, Moffitt, & Jones (2021) use Michelle Fine's concept of *strong objectivity*:

> which calls researchers to interrogate our own perspectives and positionalities and actively consider who will be highlighted and silenced by our research. Rather than downplaying or minimizing the role researchers play in the social processes we study, Fine urges us to closely identify our blind spots and examine our motivations, which allows us to see where our assumptions shape the stories participants tell us in ways they did not intend.... A stance of strong objectivity can help us better and more accurately hear and see the lived experiences of others while recognizing the structures that give rise to those experiences, especially in cases of resistance to hegemonic societal narratives. (p. 49)

This kind of strong objectivity, or reflexivity, is standard practice in qualitative work (e.g., Levitt et al., 2018; see also see also Humphreys, Lewis, Sender, & Won, 2021). The fact that it is *not even discussed* as relevant or important to quantitative work suggests that we *think* we cannot be biased in quantitative science. What folly! We are never "positionless" observers (Salter & Adams, 2013).

So as researchers, we can choose to embrace the reality of our biases and to be transparent about the lack of neutrality in our work. We can also choose to be intentional—what Rogers (in press) calls "radical intentionality"—in our efforts to change inequitable and oppressive systems in terms of who we include on our research teams, the questions we ask, the materials we use, the participants we recruit, the analyses we conduct, the interpretations we offer, and the processes of dissemination we choose to employ. Each of these decisions has a value attached to it, whether we recognize it or not, a value that upholds, challenges, or resists the status quo. To recruit the same types of participants, from the same places, to use the same materials decade after decade, the same methods, to publish in the same journals, is not unbiased work. To do work in a way that maintains inequitable systems is not unbiased work. Transparency about our biases does not make our science less rigorous. It makes our science more honest.

REFERENCES

Abaied, J. L., & Perry, S. P. (2021). Socialization of racial ideology by White parents. *Cultural Diversity and Ethnic Minority Psychology, 27*(3), 431–440. https://doi.org/10.1037/cdp0000454

Adams, G., Estrada-Villalta, S., Sullivan, D., & Markus, H. R. (2019). The psychology of neoliberalism and the neoliberalism of psychology. *Journal of Social Issues, 75*(1), 189–216. https://doi.org/10.1111/josi.12305

Adichie, C. (2009). The danger of a single story. You Tube. https://www.youtube.com/watch?v=D9Ihs241zeg

Adler, J. M. (2012). Living into the story: Agency and coherence in a longitudinal study of narrative identity development and mental health over the course of psychotherapy. *Journal of Personality and Social Psychology, 102*(2), 367–389. https://doi.org/10.1037/a0025289

Adler, J. M. (2018). Bringing the (disabled) body to personality psychology: A case study of Samantha. *Journal of Personality, 86*(5), 803–824. https://doi.org/10.1111/jopy.12364

Adler, J. M. (2019). Stability and change in narrative identity: Introduction to the special issue on repeated narration. *Qualitative Psychology, 6*(2), 134–145. https://doi.org/10.1037/qup0000155

Adler, J. M., Lakmazaheri, A., O'Brien, E., Palmer, A., Reid, M., & Tawes, E. (2021). Identity integration in people with acquired disabilities: A qualitative study. *Journal of Personality, 89*(1), 84–112. https://doi.org/10.1111/jopy.12533

Adler, J. M., Lodi-Smith, J., Philippe, F. L., & Houle, I. (2016). The incremental validity of narrative identity in predicting well-being: A review of the field and recommendations for the future. *Personality and Social Psychology Review, 20*(2), 142–175. https://doi.org/10.1177/1088868315585068

Adler, J. M., Manning, R. B. M., Hennein, R., Winschel, J., Baldari, A., Bogart, K. R., ... Wang, K. (2022). Narrative identity among people with disabilities during the COVID-19 pandemic: The interdependent self. *Journal of Research in Personality, 101*, 104302. https://doi.org/10.1016/j.jrp.2022.104302

Ainsworth, M. D. S., Blehar, M. C., Waters, E., & Wall, S. (1978). *Patterns of attachment: A psychological study of the strange situation*. Mahwah, NJ: Erlbaum.

REFERENCES

Alexander, M. (2010). *The New Jim Crow: Mass incarceration in the age of colorblindness*. New York, NY: New Press.

Anderson, L. A., O'Brien, C. M., & Owen, M. T. (2021). "The talk" and parenting while black in America: Centering race, resistance, and refuge. *Journal of Black Psychology, 48*(3–4), 475–506. https://doi.org/10.1177/00957984211034294

Andrews, M. (2002). Introduction: Counter-narratives and the power to oppose. *Narrative Inquiry, 12*, 1–6.

Andrews. T. (2022, March 9). The dogged endurance of "Law and Order." *Washington Post*. https://www.washingtonpost.com/arts-entertainment/2022/03/09/law-and-order-returns/

Arshad, M., & Chung, J. M. (2022). Practical recommendations for considering culture, race, and ethnicity in personality psychology. *Social and Personality Psychology Compass, 16*(2), e12656.

Bakker, M., van Dijk, A., & Wicherts, J. M. (2012). The rules of the game called psychological science. *Perspectives on Psychological Science, 7*(6), 543–554. https://doi.org/10.1177/1745691612459060r

Bañales, J., & Rivas-Drake, D. (2022). Showing up: A theoretical model of anti-racist identity and action for Latinx youth. *Journal of Research on Adolescence, 32*(3), 999–1019.

Bartlett, F. W. (1932). *Remembering: A study in experimental and social psychology*. Cambridge, England: Cambridge University Press.

Bauer, J. J. (2021). *The transformative self: Personal growth, narrative identity, and the good life*. New York, NY: Oxford.

Bauer, P. J., Tasdemir-Ozdes, A., & Larkina, M. (2014). Adults' reports of their earliest memories: Consistency in events, ages, and narrative characteristics over time. *Consciousness and Cognition: An International Journal, 27*, 76–88. https://doi.org/10.1016/j.concog.2014.04.008

Baumeister, R. F., Stillwell, A., & Wotman, S. R. (1990). Victim and perpetrator accounts of interpersonal conflict: Autobiographical narratives about anger. *Journal of Personality and Social Psychology, 59*, 994–1005. https://doi.org/10.1037/0022-3514.59.5.994

Berntsen, D., & Rubin, D. C. (2004). Cultural life scripts structure recall from autobiographical memory. *Memory & Cognition, 32*(3), 427–442. https://doi.org/10.3758/BF03195836

Bessi, A., Coletto, M., Davidescu, G. A., Scala, A., Caldarelli, G., & Quattrociocchi, W. (2015). Science vs conspiracy: Collective narratives in the age of misinformation. *PloS ONE, 10*(2). https://doi.org/10.1371/journal.pone.0118093

Blackie, L. E. R., & McLean, K. C. Unpublished data. *The Dating Diaries Project*.

Blackie, L. E. R., & McLean, K. C. (2022). Examining the longitudinal associations between repeated narration of recent transgressions within individuals' romantic relationships and character growth in empathy, humility, and compassion. *European Journal of Personality, 36*(4), 507–528. https://doi.org/10.1177%2F08902070211028696

Blackie, L., Weststrate, N. M., Turner, K., Adler, J., & McLean, K. C. (2023). Broadening our understanding of adversarial growth: The contribution of narrative methods. *Journal of Research in Personality*.

REFERENCES

Blagov, P. S., & Singer, J. A. (2004). Four dimensions of self-defining memories (specificity, meaning, content, and affect) and their relationships to self-restraint, distress, and repressive defensiveness. *Journal of Personality, 72*, 481–511. https://doi.org/10.1111/j.0022-3506.2004.00270.x

Blount-Hill, K., & Ajil, A. (2023). In our experience: Recognizing and challenging cognitive imperialism. In A. Aliverti, A. Chamberlen, H. Carvalho, & M. Sozzo (Eds.), *Decolonising the criminal question: Colonial legacies, contemporary problems* (pp. 329–346). Oxford, England: Oxford University Press.

Blount-Hill, K.-L., & St. John, V. J. (2017). Manufactured "mismatch": Cultural incongruence and Black experience in the academy. *Race and Justice, 7*(2), 110–126. https://doi.org/10.1177%2F0032885519877402

Blount-Hill, K.-L., St. John, V., Moton, L. N., & Ajil, A. (2022). In their experience: A review of racial and sexual minority experience in academe and proposals for building an inclusive criminology. *Race and Justice, 12*(3), 457–480. https://doi.org/10.1177/21533687221087352

Bluck, S., & Alea, N. (2009). Thinking and talking about the past: Why remember? *Applied Cognitive Psychology, 23*, 1089–1104. https://psycnet.apa.org/doi/10.1002/acp.1612

Booker, J. A., Brakke, K., Sales, J. M., & Fivush, R. (2022). Narrative identity across multiple autobiographical episodes: Considering means and variability with well-being. *Self and Identity, 21*(3), 339–362. https://doi.org/10.1080/15298868.2021.1895301

Booker, J. A., Fivush, R., & Graci, M. E. (2021). Narrative identity informs psychological adjustment: Considering three themes captured across five time points and two event valences. *Journal of Personality, 90*(3), 324–342. https://doi.org/10.1111/jopy.12668

Bowlby, J. (1969). *Attachment and loss: Volume 1. Attachment.* New York, NY: Basic Books.

Bradford, N. J., & Syed, M. (2019). Transnormativity and transgender identity development: A master narrative approach. *Sex Roles: A Journal of Research, 81*(5–6), 306–325. https://doi.org/10.1007/s11199-018-0992-7

Breen, A. V., Lewis, S. P., & Sutherland, O. (2013). Brief report: Non-suicidal self-injury in the context of self and identity development. *Journal of Adult Development, 20*(1), 57–62. https://psycnet.apa.org/doi/10.1007/s10804-013-9156-8

Brennan, C. L., Swartout, K. M., Cook, S. L., & Parrott, D. J. (2018). A qualitative analysis of offenders' emotional responses to perpetrating sexual assault. *Sexual Abuse: Journal of Research and Treatment, 30*(4), 393–412. https://doi.org/10.1177/1079063216667917

Bretherton, I. (1992). The origins of attachment theory: John Bowlby and Mary Ainsworth. *Developmental Psychology, 28*(5), 759–775. https://doi.org/10.1037/0012-1649.28.5.759

Bringmann, L. F., Elmer, T., & Eronen, M. I. (2022). Back to basics: The importance of conceptual clarification in psychological science. *Current Directions in Psychological Science, 31*(4), 340–346. https://doi.org/10.1177%2F09637214221096485

Bronfenbrenner, U. (1979). *The ecology of human development.* Cambridge, MA: Harvard University Press.

Burgoyne, A. P., Hambrick, D. Z., & Macnamara, B. N. (2020). How firm are the foundations of mind-set theory? The claims appear stronger than the evidence. *Psychological Science, 31*(3), 258–267. https://doi.org/10.1177%2F0956797619897588

Cammarota, J., & Fine, M. (2008). *Revolutionizing education: Youth participatory action research in motion*. New York, NY: Routledge.

Cerulo, K. A., & Ruane, J. M. (2014). Apologies of the rich and famous: Cultural, cognitive, and social explanations of why we care and why we forgive. *Social Psychology Quarterly, 77*(2), 123–149. https://doi.org/10.1177/0190272514530412

Chae, D., Rogers, L. O., & Yip, T. (2020). Most white parents don't talk about racism with their kids. Retrieved from https://theconversation.com/most-white-parents-dont-talk-about-racismwith-their-kids-140894

Chandler, M. J., Lalonde, C. E., Sokol, B. W., & Hallett, D. (2003). Personal persistence, identity development, and suicide: A study of Native and non-Native North American adolescents. *Monographs of The Society for Research in Child Development, 68*.

Chopik, W. J., Kelley, W. L., Vie, L. L., Lester, P. B., Bonett, D. G., Lucas, R. E., & Seligman, E. P. M. (2021). Individual and experiential predictors of character development across the deployment cycle. *European Journal of Personality, 36*(4), 597–615. https://doi.org/10.1177%2F08902070211012931

Cikara, M., Martinez, J., & Lewis, N. A., Jr. (2022). Moving beyond social categories by incorporating context more deeply in social psychological theory. *Nature Reviews Psychology, 1*, 537–549.

Cinelli, M., Brugnoli, E., Schmidt, A. L., Zollo, F., Quattrociocchi, W., & Scala, A. (2020). Selective exposure shapes the Facebook news diet. *PLoS One, 15*(3). https://doi.org/10.1371/journal.pone.0229129

Cobb, J. (2021, August 19). A warning ignored. *New York Review of Books*.

Cohler, B. J. (1982). Personal narrative and life course. In P. Baltes & O. G. Brim (Eds.), *Life span development and behavior* (Vol. 4, pp. 205–241). New York, NY: Academic Press.

Credé, M., Tynan, M. C., & Harms, P. D. (2017). Much ado about grit: A meta-analytic synthesis of the grit literature. *Journal of Personality and Social Psychology, 113*(3), 492–511. https://doi.org/10.1037/pspp0000102

Crossing, A. E., Gumudavelly, D., Watkins, N., Logue, C., & Anderson, R. E. (2022). A Critical Race Theory of Psychology as Praxis: Proposing and Utilizing Principles of PsyCrit. *Journal of Adolescent Research, 0*(0). https://doi.org/10.1177/07435584221101930Cushman, P. (1990). Why the self is empty. Toward a historically situated psychology. *American Psychologist, 45*(5), 599–611. https://psycnet.apa.org/doi/10.1037/0003-066X.45.5.599

Cushman, P. (1996). *Constructing the self, constructing America: A cultural history of psychotherapy*. Boston, MA: Da Capo Press.

Davis, L. J. (2017). Introduction: Disability, normality, and power. In L. J. Davis (Ed.), *The disability studies reader* (5th ed., pp. 1–16). New York, NY: Routledge.

Delgado, A. E., Gumudavelly, D., Watkins, N., Logue, C., & Anderson, R. E. (2022). A critical race theory of psychology as praxis: Proposing and utilizing principles of PsyCrit. *Journal of Adolescent Research*. https://doi.org/10.1177%2F07435584221101930

Delgado, R., & Stefancic, J. (Eds.). (2000). *Critical race theory: The cutting edge*. Philadelphia, PA: Temple University Press.

Delker, B. C. (2021). Interpersonal violence in context: A call to consider cultural stigma in theory and research on the psychology of trauma. In K. C. McLean (Ed.), *Cultural

REFERENCES

methods in psychology: Describing and transforming cultures. New York, NY: Oxford University Press.

Delker, B. C., Czopp, A. M., Brown, A., Fogel, C., Means, K., Patterson, A., . . . McLean, K. C. (under review). *Perceptions of sexual assault perpetrators, victims, and event depend on system justification beliefs and perpetrator atonement.*

Delker, B. C., Salton, R., & McLean, K. C. (2020). Giving voice to silence: Empowerment and disempowerment in the developmental shift from trauma "victim" to "survivor-advocate." *Journal of Trauma & Dissociation, 21*(2), 242–263. https://doi.org/10.1080/15299732.2019.1678212

Delker, B. C., Salton, R., McLean, K. C., & Syed, M. (2020). Who has to tell their trauma story and how hard will it be? Influence of cultural stigma and narrative redemption on the storying of sexual violence. *PLoS ONE, 15*(6), 1–21. https://doi.org/10.1371/journal.pone.0234201

Del Vicario, M., Bessi, A., Zollo, F., Petroni, F., Scala, A., Caldarelli, G., . . . Quattrociocchi, W. (2016). The spreading of misinformation online. *PNAS Proceedings of the National Academy of Sciences of the United States of America, 113*(3), 554–559. https://doi.org/10.1073/pnas.1517441113

Demorest, A., Popovska, A., & Dabova, M. (2012). The role of scripts in personal consistency and individual differences. *Journal of Personality, 80*(1), 187–218. https://doi.org/10.1111/j.1467-6494.2011.00727.x

Deyhle, D., & Swisher, K. (1997). Research in American Indian and Alaska Native education. In M. W. Apple (Ed.), *Review of research in education* (Vol. 22, pp. 113–194). Washington, DC: American Educational Research Association.

Drivdahl, S. B., & Hyman, I. E., Jr. (2014). Fluidity in autobiographical memories: Relationship memories sampled on two occasions. *Memory, 22*(8), 1070–1081. https://doi.org/10.1080/09658211.2013.866683

Elliot, A. (2021, September 28). When Dasani left home: What happens when trying to escape poverty means separating form your family at 13? *New York Times Magazine.* https://www.nytimes.com/2021/09/28/magazine/dasani-invisible-child.html

Equal Justice Initiative. (2019, December 9). Racial double standard in drug laws persists today. https://eji.org/news/racial-double-standard-in-drug-laws-persists-today/

Erikson, E. H. (1950). *Childhood and society.* New York, NY: Norton.

Erikson, E. H. (1968). *Identity: Youth and crisis.* New York, NY: Norton.

Eriksson, P. L., McLean, K. C., & Frisén, A. (2020). Ta det onda med det goda (accepting the bad that comes with the good): A cultural framework for identity narratives of difficult experiences in Sweden. *Identity, 20*(3), 157–169. https://psycnet.apa.org/doi/10.1080/15283488.2020.1781636

Farrow, R. (2019). *Catch and kill: Lies, spies, and a conspiracy to protect predators.* Ashland, OR: Hachette.

Ferguson, C. J., & Heene, M. (2012). A vast graveyard of undead theories: Publication bias and psychological science's aversion to the null. *Perspectives on Psychological Science, 7*(6), 555–561. https://doi.org/10.1177%2F1745691612459059

Ferré-Sadurní, L. (2019, July 2). Teenager accused of rape deserves leniency because he's from a "good family," judge says. *New York Times.* https://www.nytimes.com/2019/07/02/nyregion/judge-james-troiano-rape.html

Fish, J. (2022). Towards a Haudenosaunee developmental science: Perspectives from the Two Row Wampum. *Infant and Child Development*, *31*(1), e2279. https://doi.org/10.1002/icd.2279

Fish, J., & Counts, P. K. (2021). Justice for Native people, justice for Native me. In K. C. McLean (Ed.), *Cultural methods in psychology: Describing and transforming cultures*. New York, NY: Oxford University Press. https://doi.org/10.1093/oso/9780190095949.003.0008

Fish, J., Counts, P. K., Ruzzicone, D. J., Ogbeide, I. E., & Syed, M. (2023). ". . . Inside of my home, I was getting a full dose of culture": Exploring the ecology of Native Peoples' development through stories. *American Journal of Orthopsychiatry*. Advance online publication. https://doi.org/10.1037/ort0000690

Fish, J., & Syed, M. (2018). Native Americans in higher education: An ecological systems perspective. *Journal of College Student Development*, *59*(4), 387–403. https://doi.org/10.1353/csd.2018.0038

Fivush, R. (2004). Voice and silence: A feminist model of autobiographical memory. In J. M. Lucariello, J. A. Hudson, R. Fivush, & P. J. Bauer (Eds.), *The development of the mediated mind: Sociocultural context and cognitive development* (pp. 79–99). Mahwah, NJ: Erlbaum.

Fivush, R. (2010). Speaking silence: the social construction of silence in autobiographical and cultural narratives. *Memory*, *18*(2), 88–98. https://doi.org/10.1080/09658210903029404

Fivush, R. (2011). The development of autobiographical memory. *Annual Review of Psychology*, *62*, 559–582. https://doi.org/10.1146/annurev.psych.121208.131702

Fivush, R. (2019). *Family narratives and the development of an autobiographical self: Social and cultural perspectives on autobiographical memory*. New York, NY: Routledge/Taylor & Francis. https://doi.org/10.4324/9780429029158

Fivush, R, Haden, C. A., & Reese, E. (2006). Elaborating on elaborations: Role of maternal reminiscing style in cognitive and socioemotional development. *Child Development*, *77*, 1568–1588. https://www.jstor.org/stable/4139261

Fivush, R., & Reese, E. (2002). Reminiscing and relating: The development of parent-child talk about the past. In J. D. Webster & B. K. Haight (Eds.), *Critical advances in reminiscence work: From theory to application* (pp. 109–122). New York, NY: Springer.

Fox, M., & Fine, M. (2013). Accountable to whom? A critical science counter-story about a city that stopped caring for its young. *Children & Society*, *27*(4), 321–335. https://doi.org/10.1111/chso.12031

Fraley, R. C., & Brumbaugh, C. C. (2004). A dynamical systems approach to conceptualizing and studying stability and change in attachment security. In W. S. Rholes & J. A. Simpson (Eds.), *Adult attachment: Theory, research, and clinical implications* (pp. 86–132). New York, NY: Guilford Press.

Fraley, R. C., Gillath, O., & Deboeck, P. R. (2021). Do life events lead to enduring changes in adult attachment styles? A naturalistic longitudinal investigation. *Journal of Personality and Social Psychology*, *120*(6), 1567–1606. https://doi.org/10.1037/pspi0000326

Frazier, P., Tennen, H., Gavian, M., Park, C., Tomich, P., & Tashiro, T. (2009). Does self-reported Posttraumatic growth reflect genuine positive change? *Psychological Science*, *20*(7), 912–919. https://www.jstor.org/stable/40575117

REFERENCES

French, B. H., Lewis, J. A., Mosley, D. V., Adames, H. Y., Chavez-Dueñas, N. Y., Chen, G. A., & Neville, H. A. (2020). Toward a psychological framework of radical healing in communities of color. *The Counseling Psychologist, 48*(1), 14–46. https://doi.org/10.1177%2F0011000019843506

Fricker, M. (2007). *Epistemic injustice: Power and the ethics of knowing.* New York, NY: Oxford University Press. https://doi.org/10.1093/acprof:oso/9780198237907.001.0001

Friedman, L. J. (1999). *Identity's architect: A biography of Erik H. Erikson.* Cambridge, MA: Harvard University Press.

Friese, M., & Frankenbach, J. (2020). p-Hacking and publication bias interact to distort meta-analytic effect size estimates. *Psychological Methods, 25*(4), 456–471. https://doi.org/10.1037/met0000246

Fryberg, S. A., Markus, H. R., Oyserman, D., & Stone, J. M. (2008). Of warrior chiefs and Indian princesses: The psychological consequences of American Indian mascots. *Basic and Applied Social Psychology, 30*, 208–218. https://psycnet.apa.org/doi/10.1080/01973530802375003

Fryberg, S. A., & Townsend, S. S. M. (2008). The psychology of invisibility. In G. Adams, M. Biernat, N. R. Branscombe, C. S. Crandall, & L. S. Wrightsman (Eds.), *Decade of behavior. Commemorating Brown: The social psychology of racism and discrimination* (pp. 173–193). Washington, DC: American Psychological Association. https://doi.org/10.1037/11681-010

García Coll, C., Lamberty, G., Jenkins, R., McAdoo, H. P., Crnic, K., Wasik, B. H., & Vázquez García, H. (1996). An integrative model for the study of developmental competencies in minority children. *Child Development, 67*(5), 1891–1914. https://doi.org/10.1111/j.1467-8624.1996.tb01834.x

Garland Thomson, R. (2013). Disability studies: A field emerged. *American Quarterly, 65*, 915–926. https://doi.org/10.1353/aq.2013.0052

GBD 2019 Police Violence US Subnational Collaborators. (2021). Fatal police violence by race and state in the USA, 1980–2019: A network meta-regression. *Lancet, 398*, 1239–1255. https://www.thelancet.com/journals/lancet/article/PIIS0140-6736(21)01609-3/fulltext

Giddens, A. (1991). *Modernity and self-identity.* Cambridge, England: Polity Press.

Gill, R., & Orgad, S. (2018). The amazing bounce-backable woman: Resilience and the psychological turn in neoliberalism. *Sociological Research Online, 23*(2), 477–495. https://doi.org/10.1177%2F1360780418769673

Gilligan, C. (2011). *Joining the resistance.* Cambridge, England: Polity Press.

Gilligan, C. (2015). The Listening Guide method of psychological inquiry. *Qualitative Psychology, 2*, 69–77. https://doi.org/10.1037/qup0000023

Haalen, J. (2010). *Hard knocks: Domestic violence and the psychology of storytelling.* London, England: Routledge.

Habermas, T., & Bluck, S. (2000). Getting a life: The emergence of the life story in adolescence. *Psychological Bulletin, 126*(5), 748–69. https://psycnet.apa.org/doi/10.1037/0033-2909.126.5.748

Habermas, T., & de Silveira, C. (2008). The development of global coherence in life narratives across adolescence: Temporal, causal, and thematic aspects. *Developmental Psychology, 44*, 707–721. https://psycnet.apa.org/doi/10.1037/0012-1649.44.3.707

Hagerman, M. A. (2014). White families and race: Colour-blind and colour-conscious approaches to white racial socialization. *Ethnic and Racial Studies, 37*(14), 2598–2614. https://doi.org/10.1080/01419870.2013.848289

Hamblin, J. (2015, July 16). The paradox of effort: A medical case against too much self-control. *The Atlantic*. https://www.theatlantic.com/health/archive/2015/07/the-health-cost-of-upward-mobility/398486/

Hammack, P. L. (2008). Narrative and the cultural psychology of identity. *Personality and Social Psychology Review, 12*(3), 222–247. https://doi.org/10.1177/1088868308316892

Hannah-Jones, N., Roper, C., Silverman, I., & Silverstein, J., (2021). *The 1619 Project: A new American origin story*. London, England: WH Allen.

Harper, S. R. (2015). Black male college achievers and resistant responses to racist stereotypes at predominantly White colleges and universities. *Harvard Educational Review, 85*(4), 646–674. https://doi-org.ezproxy.library.wwu.edu/10.17763/0017-8055.85.4.646

Hawkman, A. M. (2020). Swimming in and through whiteness: Antiracism in social studies teacher education. *Theory & Research in Social Education*, 1–28. https://doi.org/10.1080/00933104.2020.1724578

Helms, J. E. (1990). *Black and White racial identity: Theory, research, and practice*. Westport, CT: Greenwood Press.

Helms, J. E. (1993). I also said "White racial identity influences White researchers." *The Counseling Psychologist, 21*(2), 240–243. https://doi.org/10.1177/0011000093212007

Hogan, R., & Roberts, B. W. (2004). A socioanalytic model of maturity. *Journal of Career Assessment, 12*(2), 207–217. https://doi.org/10.1177/1069072703255882

hooks, b. (1990). *Yearning: Race, gender, and cultural politics*. Boston, MA: South End Press.

Hudson, N. W. (2019). Dynamics and processes in personality change interventions. In J. F. Rauthmann (Ed.), *The handbook of personality dynamics and processes* (pp. 1273–1293). San Diego, CA: Elsevier.

Hudson, N. W., Fraley, R. C., Chopik, W. J., & Briley, D. A. (2020). Change goals robustly predict trait growth: A mega-analysis of a dozen intensive longitudinal studies examining volitional change. *Social Psychological and Personality Science, 11*(6), 723–732. https://doi.org/10.1177/1948550619878423

Hughes, D., Rodriguez, J., Smith, E. P., Johnson, D. J., Stevenson, H. C., & Spicer, P. (2006). Parents' ethnic-racial socialization practices: A review of research and directions for future study. *Developmental Psychology, 42*(5), 747–770. https://doi.org/10.1037/0012-1649.42.5.747

Humphreys, L., Lewis, N. A., Sender, K., & Won, A. S. (2021). Integrating qualitative methods and open science: Five principles for more trustworthy research, *Journal of Communication, 71*(5), 855–874. https://doi.org/10.1093/joc/jqab026

Hyman, I. E. (1994). Conversational remembering: Story recall with a peer versus for an experimenter. *Applied Cognitive Psychology, 8*(1), 49–66. https://doi.org/10.1002/acp.2350080106

James, W. (1902). *The varieties of religious experience: A study in human nature*. New York, NY: Longmans, Green.

Jayawickreme, E., & Blackie, L. E. R. (2014). Post-traumatic growth as positive personality change: Evidence, controversies and future directions. *European Journal of Personality, 28*(4), 312–331. https://doi.org/10.1002/per.1963

Joe (no last name given). (2018). Red Lake Band of Ojibwe. Retrieved from https://www.originatives.org/joe-digital-story.

John, O. P., Naumann, L. P., & Soto, C. J. (2008). Paradigm shift to the integrative Big Five trait taxonomy: history, measurement, and conceptual issues. In O. P. John, R. W. Robins, & L. A. Pervin (Eds.), *Handbook of personality: Theory and research* (pp. 114–158). New York, NY: Guilford Press.

Jones, S. C. T., & Neblett, E. W. (2016). Racial–ethnic protective factors and mechanisms in psychosocial prevention and intervention programs for Black youth. *Clinical Child and Family Psychology Review, 19*(2), 134–161. https://doi.org/10.1007/s10567-016-0201-6

Jones, S. C. T., & Neblett, E. W., Jr. (2019). The impact of racism on the mental health of people of color. In M. T. Williams, D. C. Rosen, & J. W. Kanter (Eds.), *Eliminating race-based mental health disparities: Promoting equity and culturally responsive care across settings* (pp. 79–97). Oakland, CA: Context Press.

Josselson, R. (2009). The present of the past: Dialogues with memory over time. *Journal of Personality, 77*(3), 647–668. https://doi.org/10.1111/j.1467-6494.2009.00560.x

Josselson, R. (2013). *Interviewing for qualitative inquiry: A relational approach*. New York, NY: Guilford Press.

Jost, J. T., Langer, M., Badaan, V., Azevedo, F., Etchezahar, E., Ungaretti, J., & Hennes, E. P. (2017). Ideology and the limits of self-interest: System justification motivation and conservative advantages in mass politics. *Translational Issues in Psychological Science, 3*(3), e1–e26. https://doi.org/10.1037/tps0000127

Kantor, J., & Twohey, M. (2019). *She said: Breaking the sexual harassment story that helped ignite a movement*. New York, NY: Penguin.

Kasser, T., Cohn, S., Kanner, A. D., & Ryan, R. M. (2007). Some costs of American corporate capitalism: A psychological exploration of value and goal conflicts. *Psychological Inquiry, 18*(1), 1–22. https://doi.org/10.1080/10478400701386579

Katsiaficas, D. (2021). Participatory action research with immigrant-origin youth. In K. C. McLean (Ed.), *Cultural methods in psychology: Describing and transforming cultures*. New York, NY: Oxford University Press. https://doi.org/10.1093/oso/9780190095949.003.0009,

Khan, F., Chong, J. Y., Theisen, J. C., Fraley, R. C., Young, J. F., & Hankin, B. L. (2020). Development and change in attachment: A multiwave assessment of attachment and its correlates across childhood and adolescence. *Journal of Personality and Social Psychology, 118*(6), 1188–1206. https://doi.org/10.1037/pspi0000211

Kiper, G., Atari, M., Yan, V. X., & Oyserman, D. (2022, January 22). The upside: How people make sense of difficulty matters in a crisis. https://doi.org/10.31234/osf.io/gy5pd

Klimstra, T. A., & McLean, K. C. (2023). The importance of contextualism for the study of personality development: It is time to revisit personality "maturation" and "the healthy personality." Manuscript under review.

Knight, J. L., Giuliano, T. A., & Sanchez-Ross, M. G. (2001). Famous or infamous? The influence of celebrity status and race on perceptions of responsibility for rape. *Basic and Applied Social Psychology, 23*(3), 183–190. https://doi.org/10.1207/S15324834BASP2303_4

Köber, C., & Habermas, T. (2017). How stable is the personal past? Stability of most important autobiographical memories and life narratives across eight years in a life span sample. *Journal of Personality and Social Psychology, 113*(4), 608–626. https://psycnet.apa.org/doi/10.1037/pspp0000145

Köber, C., Schmiedek, F., & Habermas, T. (2015). Characterizing lifespan development of three aspects of coherence in life narratives: A cohort-sequential study. *Developmental Psychology, 51*(2), 260–275. https://doi.org/10.1037/a0038668

Labov, W., & Waletzky, J. (1967). Narrative analysis: Oral versions of personal experience. In I. Helm (Ed.), *Essays on the verbal and visual arts: Proceedings of the 1966 annual spring meeting of the American ethnological society* (pp. 12–44). Seattle, WA: University of Washington Press.

Lamade, R. V., Jayawickreme, E., Blackie, L. E. R., & McGrath, R. E. (2020). Are sequential sample designs useful for examining post-traumatic changes in character strengths? *Journal of Positive Psychology, 15*(3), 292–299. https://doi.org/10.1080/17439760.2019.1610481

Langhout, R. D., Drake, P., & Rosselli, F. (2009). Classism in the university setting: Examining student antecedents and outcomes. *Journal of Diversity in Higher Education, 2*, 166–181. https://psycnet.apa.org/doi/10.1037/a0016209

Ledgerwood, A., Hudson, S. T. J., Lewis, N. A., Jr., Maddox, K. B., Pickett, C. L., Remedios, J. D., . . . Wilkins, C. L. (2022). The pandemic as a portal: Reimagining psychological science as truly open and inclusive. *Perspectives on Psychological Science.* https://doi.org/10.1177/17456916211036654

Leighton, S. (2016, September 1). Driving while affluent: A richly unjust defense. *Legal Reader.* https://www.legalreader.com/driving-while-affluent-a-richly-unjust-defense/

Lerner, R. M. (2006). Developmental science, developmental systems, and contemporary theories of human development. In R. M. Lerner & W. Damon (Eds.), *Handbook of child psychology: Theoretical models of human development* (pp. 1–17). Hoboken, NJ: John Wiley & Sons.

Levitt, H. M., Bamberg, M., Creswell, J. W., Frost, D. M., Josselson, R., & Suárez-Orozco, C. (2018). Journal article reporting standards for qualitative primary, qualitative meta-analytic, and mixed methods research in psychology: The APA Publications and Communications Board task force report. *American Psychologist, 73*(1), 26–46. https://doi.org/10.1037/amp0000151

Lewis, N. A., Jr. (2021). What counts as good science? How the battle for methodological legitimacy affects public psychology. *American Psychologist, 76*(8), 1323–1333. https://psycnet.apa.org/doi/10.1037/amp0000870

Li, Y., & Bates, T. C. (2019). You can't change your basic ability, but you work at things, and that's how we get hard things done: Testing the role of growth mindset on response to setbacks, educational attainment, and cognitive ability. *Journal of Experimental Psychology: General, 148*(9), 1640–1655. https://doi.org/10.1037/xge0000669

Lilgendahl, J. P., McLean, K. C., & Mansfield, C. D. (2013). When is meaning making unhealthy for the self? The roles of neuroticism, implicit theories, and memory telling in trauma and transgression memories. *Memory, 21*(1), 79–96. https://doi.org/10.1080/09658211.2012.706615

REFERENCES

Loyd, A. B., & Gaither, S. E. (2018). Racial/ethnic socialization for White youth: What we know and future directions. *Journal of Applied Developmental Psychology, 59*, 54–64. https://doi.org/10.1016/j.appdev.2018.05.004

Lucas, R. E., & Donnellan, M. B. (2011). Personality development across the life span: Longitudinal analyses with a national sample from Germany. *Journal of Personality and Social Psychology, 101*(4), 847–861. https://doi.org/10.1037/a0024298

Luyckx, K., Goossens, L., & Soenens, B. (2006). A developmental contextual perspective on identity construction in emerging adulthood: Change dynamics in commitment formation and commitment evaluation. *Developmental Psychology, 42*(2), 366–380. https://doi.org/10.1037/0012-1649.42.2.366

Mackinnon, S. P., De Pasquale, D., & Pratt, M. W. (2016). Predicting generative concern in young adulthood from narrative intimacy: A 5-year follow-up. *Journal of Adult Development, 23*, 27–35. https://doi.org/10.1007/s10804-015-9218-1

Macnamara, B. N., & Burgoyne, A. P. (2022). Do growth mindset interventions impact students' academic achievement? A systematic review and meta-analysis with recommendations for best practices. *Psychological Bulletin*. https://doi.org/10.1037/bul0000352

Mansfield, C. D., McLean, K. C., & Lilgendahl, J. P. (2010). Narrating traumas and transgressions: Links between narrative processing, wisdom, and well-being. *Narrative Inquiry, 20*(2), 246–273. https://psycnet.apa.org/doi/10.1075/ni.20.2.02man

Mansfield, C. D., Pasupathi, M., & McLean, K. C. (2015). Is narrating growth in stories of personal transgressions associated with increased well-being, self-compassion, and forgiveness of others? *Journal of Research in Personality, 58*, 69–83. https://doi.org/10.1016/j.jrp.2015.05.008

Mansfield, C. D., Pasupathi, M., & McLean, K. C. (2022). The challenges of the experimental paradigm in narrative identity research. *Journal of Research in Personality.*

Marcia, J. E. (1966). Development and validation of ego-identity status. *Journal of Personality and Social Psychology, 3*(5), 551–558. https://doi.org/10.1037/h0023281

Markus, H. R., & Kitayama, S. (1991). Culture and the self: Implications for cognition, emotion, and motivation. *Psychological Review, 98*(2), 224–253. https://doi.org/10.1037/0033-295X.98.2.224

Maruna, S. (2001). *Making good: How ex-convicts reform and rebuild their lives.* Washington, DC: American Psychological Association. https://doi.org/10.1037/10430-000

Maruna, S., & Ramsden, D. (2004). Living to tell the tale: Redemption narratives, shame management, and offender rehabilitation. In A. Lieblich, D. P. McAdams, & R. Josselson (Eds.), *Healing plots: The narrative basis of psychotherapy* (pp. 129–149). Washington, DC: American Psychological Association. https://doi.org/10.1037/10682-007

Maruna, S., Wilson, L., & Curran, K. (2006). Why God is often found behind bars: Prison conversions and the crisis of self-narrative. *Research in Human Development, 3*(2–3), 161–184. https://doi.org/10.1207/s15427617rhd0302&3_6

McAdams, D. P. (1988). *Power, intimacy, and the life story: Personological inquiries into identity.* New York, NY: Guilford Press.

McAdams, D. P. (1993). The *stories we live by: Personal myths and the making of the self.* New York, NY: Guilford Press.

McAdams, D. P. (1995). What do we know when we know a person? *Journal of Personality*, 63, 365–396. https://psycnet.apa.org/doi/10.1111/j.1467-6494.1995.tb00500.x

McAdams, D. P. (2001). The psychology of life stories. *Review of General Psychology*, 5, 100–122. https://psycnet.apa.org/doi/10.1037/1089-2680.5.2.100

McAdams, D. P. (2006). *The redemptive self: Stories Americans live by*. New York, NY: Oxford University Press. https://doi.org/10.1093/acprof:oso/9780195176933.001.0001

McAdams, D. P. (2015). *The art and science of personality development*. New York, NY: Guilford Press.

McAdams, D. P., Anyidoho, N. A., Brown, C., Huang, Y. T., Kaplan, B., & Machado, M. A. (2004). Traits and stories: Links between dispositional and narrative features of personality. *Journal of Personality*, 72, 761–784. https://doi.org/10.1111/j.0022-3506.2004.00279.x

McAdams, D. P., Bauer, J. J., Sakaeda, A. R., Anyi-doho, N. A., Machado, M. A., Magrino-Failla, K., White, K. W., & Pals, J. L. (2006). Continuity and change in the life story: A longitudinal study of autobiographical memories in emerging adulthood. *Journal of Personality*, 74, 1371–1400. http://dx.doi.org/10.1111/j.1467-6494.2006.00412.x

McAdams, D. P., & Guo, J. (2015). Narrating the generative life. *Psychological Science*, 26(4), 475–483. https://doi.org/10.1177/0956797614568318

McAdams, D. P., & Manczak, E. (2015). Personality and the life story. In M. Mikulincer & P. R. Shaver (Eds.), *APA handbook of personality and social psychology, Volume 4: Personality processes and individual differences* (pp. 425–446). Washington, DC: American Psychological Association. https://doi.org/10.1037/14343-019

McAdams, D. P., & McLean, K. C. (2013). Narrative identity. *Current Directions in Psychological Science*, 22(3), 233–238. https://doi.org/10.1177/0963721413475622

McAdams, D. P., & Pals, J. L. (2006). A new Big Five: Fundamental principles for an integrative science of personality. *American Psychologist*, 61(3), 204–217. https://doi.org/10.1037/0003-066X.61.3.204

McClelland, S. I. (2017). Vulnerable listening: Possibilities and challenges of doing qualitative research. *Qualitative Psychology*, 4(3), 338–352. https://doi.org/10.1037/qup0000068

McCrae, R. R., & Costa, P. T., Jr. (2004). A contemplated revision of the NEO Five-Factor Inventory. *Personality and Individual Differences*, 36, 587–596. http://dx.doi.org/10.1016/S0191-8869(03)00118-1

McCrae, R. R., & Costa, P. T., Jr. (2008). The five-factor theory of personality. In O. P. John, R. W. Robins, & L. A. Pervin (Eds.), *Handbook of personality: Theory and research* (3rd ed., pp. 159–181). New York, NY: Guilford Press.

McLean, K. C. (2016). *The co-authored self: Family stories and the construction of personal identity*. New York, NY: Oxford University Press.

McLean, K. C., Breen, A., & Fournier, M. A. (2010). Constructing the self in early, middle, and late adolescent boys: Narrative identity, individuation, and well-being. *Journal of Research on Adolescence*, 20, 166–187. https://doi.org/10.1111/j.1532-7795.2009.00633.x

McLean, K. C., Delker, B., Dunlop, W. L., Salton, R., & Syed, M. (2020). Redemptive stories and those who tell them are preferred in the US. *Collabra*, 6(1), 39. https://doi.org/10.1525/collabra.369

McLean, K. C., Dunlap, D., Jennings, S. C., Litvitskiy, N. S., & Lilgendahl, J. P. (2021). Stability and change in autobiographical reasoning: A four-year longitudinal study of narrative identity development. *Journal of Personality*. https://psycnet.apa.org/doi/10.1111/jopy.12669

McLean, K. C., Fish, J., Rogers, L. O., & Syed. M. (2023). Integrating Systems of Power and Privilege in the Study of Resilience. *American Psychologist*.

McLean, K. C., Köber, C., & Haraldsson, K. G. (2019). The repeated narration of specific events and identity stability in midlife. *Qualitative Psychology*, 6(2), 146–155. https://doi.org/10.1037/qup0000154

McLean, K. C., Koepf, I. M., & Lilgendahl, J. P. (2022). Identity development and major choice among underrepresented students interested in STEM majors: A longitudinal qualitative analysis. *Emerging Adulthood*, 10(2), 386–401. https://doi.org/10.1177%2F21676968211015549

McLean, K. C., Lilgendahl, J. P., Fordham, C., Alpert, E., Marsden, E., Szymanowski, K., & McAdams, D. P. (2018). Identity development in cultural context: The role of deviating from master narratives. *Journal of Personality*, 86(4), 631–651. https://psycnet.apa.org/doi/10.1111/jopy.12341

McLean, K. C., & Mansfield, C. D. (2010). To reason or not to reason: Is autobiographical reasoning always beneficial? In T. Habermas (Ed.), *New directions in child and adolescent development: The development of autobiographical reasoning in adolescence and beyond*, 131, 85–97.

McLean, K. C., & Mansfield, C. (2011). The co-construction of adolescent narrative processes: Narrative processing as a function of adolescent age, gender, and maternal scaffolding. *Developmental Psychology*, 5, 1–12. https://psycnet.apa.org/doi/10.1037/a0025563

McLean, K. C., Pasupathi, M., Greenhoot, A. F., & Fivush, R. (2017). Does intraindividual variability in narration matter and for what? *Journal of Research in Personality*, 69, 55–66. https://doi.org/10.1016/j.jrp.2016.04.003

McLean, K. C., Pasupathi, M., & Pals, J. L. (2007). Selves creating stories creating selves: A process model of narrative self development in adolescence and adulthood. *Personality and Social Psychology Review*, 11, 262–278. https://doi.org/10.1177%2F1088868307301034

McLean, K. C., & Riggs, A. E. (2022). No age differences? No problem. *Infant and Child Development*, 31(1), e2261. https://doi.org/10.1002/icd.2261

McLean, K. C., & Syed, M. (2015). Personal, master, and alternative narratives: An integrative framework for understanding identity development in context. *Human Development*, 58(6), 318–349. https://doi.org/10.1159/000445817

McLean, K. C., & Syed, M. A (2021). Different road towards a better personality science: Commentary on Leising et al. *Personality Science*.

McLean, K. C., Syed, M., Pasupathi, M., Adler, J. M., Dunlop, W. L., Drustrup, D., ... McCoy, T. P. (2020). The empirical structure of narrative identity: The initial Big Three. *Journal of Personality and Social Psychology*, 119(4), 920–944. https://doi.org/10.1037/pspp0000247

McLean, K. C., Syed, M., & Shucard, H. (2016). Bringing identity content to the fore: Links to identity development processes. *Emerging Adulthood*, 4(5), 356–364. https://doi.org/10.1177/2167696815626820

McLean, K. C., Wood, B., & Breen, A. V. (2013). Reflecting on a difficult life: Narrative construction in vulnerable adolescents. *Journal of Adolescent Research*, 28(4), 431–452. https://doi.org/10.1177/0743558413484355

McPhetres, J., & Zuckerman, M. (2017). Religious people endorse different standards of evidence when evaluating religious versus scientific claims. *Social Psychological and Personality Science, 8*(7), 836–842. https://doi.org/10.1177/1948550617691098

Merrill, N., & Fivush, R. (2016). Intergenerational narratives and identity across development. *Developmental Review, 40*, 72–92. https://doi.org/10.1016/j.dr.2016.03.001

Miller, B. L. (2016). Social class and crime. In W. Jennings, G. Higgins, M. Maldonado-Molina, & D. Khey (Eds.), *The Wiley encyclopedia of crime and punishment* (1st ed.). Hoboken, NJ: Wiley-Blackwell.

Miller, C. (2019), *Know my name: A memoir*. New York, NY: Penguin.

Miller, G. E., Yu, T., Chen, E., & Brody, G. H. (2015). Self-control forecasts better psychosocial outcomes but faster epigenetic aging in low-SES youth. *Proceedings of the National Academy of Sciences, 112*(33), 10325–10330. https://doi.org/10.1073/pnas.1505063112

Miller, W. R. (2004). The phenomenon of quantum change. *Journal of Clinical Psychology, 60*(5), 453–460. https://doi.org/10.1002/jclp.20000

Millie (no last name given). (2018). White Earth Band of Ojibwe. Retrieved from https://www.originatives.org/joe-digital-story.

Mills, M. C., & Rüttenauer, T. (2022). The effect of mandatory COVID-19 certificates on vaccine uptake: synthetic-control modelling of six countries. *Lancet Public Health, 7*(1), e15–e22. https://doi.org/10.1016/S2468-2667(21)00273-5

Mishler, E. G. (2004). Historians of the self: Restorying lives, revising identities. *Research in Human Development, 1:1-2*, 101–121. https://doi.org/10.1080/15427609.2004.9683331

Mitchell, C. E. (2021). *Narrative identity and wellbeing in mid-adolescence: The neglected middle child in narrative identity research* (Thesis, Doctor of Philosophy). University of Otago. Retrieved from http://hdl.handle.net/10523/12374

Moffitt, U., & Rogers, L. O (2022). Studying ethnic-racial identity among white youth: White supremacy as a developmental context. Journal of Research on Adolescence, *32*(3), 815–828. https://doi.org/10.1111/jora.12762.

Moffitt, U., Rogers, L. O., & Dastrup, K. R. (2021). Beyond ethnicity: Applying Helms's white racial identity development model among white youth. *Journal of Research on Adolescence, 32*(3), 1140–1159. https://doi.org/10.1111/jora.12645.

Morrison, G. Z. (2010). Two separate worlds: Students of color at a predominantly white university. *Journal of Black Studies, 40*(5), 987–1015. http://www.jstor.org/stable/4064861

Moton, L. N., & Blount-Hill, K-L. (2022). How bell hooks taught us to talk back: A love letter. *Race and Justice, 12*(3):618–619. https://doi.org/10.1177%2F21533687221101207

Munafò, M., Nosek, B., Bishop, D.,Button, K. S., Chambers, C. D., Percie du Sert, N., ... Ioannidis, J. P. A. (2017). A manifesto for reproducible science. *Nature and Human Behavior, 1*, 0021. https://doi.org/10.1038/s41562-016-0021

Nelson, K., & Fivush, R. (2004). The emergence of autobiographical memory: A social cultural developmental theory. *Psychological Review, 111*(2), 486–511. https://doi.org/10.1037/0033-295X.111.2.486

Nelson, L. H. (2001). *Damaged identities, narrative repair*. Ithaca, NY: Cornell University Press.

Nigro, G., Ross, E., Binns, T., & Kurtz, C. (2020). Apologies in the #MeToo moment. *Psychology of Popular Media, 9*(4), 403–411. https://doi.org/10.1037/ppm0000261

REFERENCES

Nosek, B. A. (2014). Improving my lab, my science with the open science framework. *APS Observer, 27*(3). https://www.psychologicalscience.org/observer/improving-my-lab-my-science-with-the-open-science-framework

Nzinga, K., Rapp, D. N., Leatherwood, C., Easterday, M., Rogers, L. O., Gallagher, N., & Medin, D. L. (2018). Should social scientists be distanced from or engaged with the people they study? *PNAS Proceedings of the National Academy of Sciences of the United States of America, 115*(45), 11435–11441. https://doi.org/10.1073/pnas.1721167115

O'Brien, T. (1990). *The things they carried*. Boston, MA: Houghton Mifflin

Onyeador, I. N., Daumeyer, N. M., Rucker, J. M., Duker, A., Kraus, M. W., & Richeson, J. A. (2021). Disrupting beliefs in racial progress: Reminders of persistent racism alter perceptions of past, but not current, racial economic equality. *Personality and Social Psychology Bulletin, 47*(5), 753–765. https://doi.org/10.1177%2F0146167220942625

O'Sullivan, J. (1845). Annexation. *The United States Magazine and Democratic Review, 17*, 5–6, 9–10.

Pals, J. L. (2006). Narrative identity processing of difficult life experiences: Pathways of personality development and positive self-transformation in adulthood. *Journal of Personality, 74*(4), 1079–1110. https://doi.org/10.1111/j.1467-6494.2006.00403.x

Pasupathi, M. (2001). The social construction of the personal past and its implications for adult development. *Psychological Bulletin, 127*(5), 651–672. https://doi.org/10.1037/0033-2909.127.5.651

Pasupathi, M. (2015). Autobiographical reasoning and my discontent: Alternative paths from narrative to identity. In K. C. McLean & M. Syed (Eds.), *The Oxford handbook of identity development* (pp. 166–181). New York, NY: Oxford University Press.

Pasupathi, M. (2021). It's past time to acknowledge that all psychology is cultural psychology. Talk presented at the virtual meetings of the Association for Research in Personality.

Pasupathi, M., Billitteri, J., Mansfield, C. D., Wainryb, C., Hanley, G. E., & Taheri, K. (2015). Regulating emotion and identity by narrating harm. *Journal of Research in Personality, 1*(58), 127–136. https://doi.org/10.1016/j.jrp.2015.07.003

Pasupathi. M., Fivush, R., Greenhoot, A. F., & McLean, K. C. (2020). Intraindividual variability in narrative identity: Complexities, garden paths, and untapped research potential. *European Journal of Personality, 34*(6), 1138–1150. https://doi.org/10.1002%2Fper.2279

Pasupathi, M., Fivush, R., & Hernandez-Martinez, M. (2016). Talking about it: Stories as paths to healing after violence. *Psychology of Violence, 6*(1), 49–56. https://doi.org/10.1037/vio0000017

Pasupathi, M., & Hoyt, T. (2009). The development of narrative identity in late adolescence and emergent adulthood: The continued importance of listeners. *Developmental Psychology, 45*(2), 558–574. https://doi.org/10.1037/a0014431

Pasupathi, M., Mansour, E., & Brubaker, J. R. (2007). Developing a life story: Constructing relations between self and experience in autobiographical narratives. *Human Development, 50*, 85–110. https://psycnet.apa.org/doi/10.1159/000100939

Pasupathi, M., McLean, K. C., Weeks, T. L., & Hynes, W. (2021). Tailoring narration for distinct audiences in emerging adulthood. *Emerging Adulthood, 9*(6), 725–736. https://doi.org/10.1177%2F2167696819856753

Pasupathi, M., & Rich, B. (2005). Inattentive listening undermines self-verification in personal storytelling. *Journal of Personality, 73*, 1051–1086. https://psycnet.apa.org/doi/10.1111/j.1467-6494.2005.00338.x

Pasupathi, M., & Wainryb, C. (2010). Developing moral agency through narrative. *Human Development, 53*, 55–80. https://www.jstor.org/stable/26764946

Pasupathi, M., & Wainryb, C. (2019). Ghosts in the story: The role of audiences in stability and change in twice-told life stories. *Qualitative Psychology, 6*(2), 178–193. https://doi.org/10.1037/qup0000153

Patterson, A. L., Dunlap, D., Payne, N. J., Peterson, A., Tiemersma, K., Turner, K., ... McLean, K. C. (2022). The role of repeated narration in identity development: The evaluation of the transition to college over time. *Qualitative Psychology, 9*(2), 171–193. https://doi.org/10.1037/qup0000234

Pen America. (2022). Banned in the USA: Rising school book bans threaten free expression and students' First Amendment rights. https://pen.org/banned-in-the-usa/

Perlin, J. D., & Fivush, R. (2021). Revisiting redemption: A life span developmental account of the functions of narrative redemption. *Human Development, 65*(1), 23–42. https://doi.org/10.1159/000514357

Perry, S. P., Skinner, A. L., & Abaied, J. L. (2019). Bias awareness predicts color conscious racial socialization methods among White parents. *Journal of Social Issues, 75*(4), 1035–1056. https://doi.org/10.1111/josi.12348

Piaget, J., & Inhelder, B. (1969). *The psychology of the child*. New York, NY: Basic Books.

Pica, E., Sheahan, C., & Pozzulo, J. (2020). "But he's a star football player!": How social status influences mock jurors' perceptions in a sexual assault case. *Journal of Interpersonal Violence, 35*(19–20), 3963–3985. https://doi.org/10.1177/0886260517713715

Presser, L., & Suzann, K. (2009). "'I got a quick tongue': Negotiating ex-convict identity in mixed company." In B. M. Veysey, J. Christian, and D. J. Martinez (Eds.), *How offenders transform their lives* (pp. 72–86). Cullompton, Devon, UK: Culmcott House.

Reese, E., Haden, C. A., Baker-Ward, L., Bauer, P., Fivush, R., & Ornstein, P. A. (2011). Coherence of personal narratives across the lifespan: A multidimensional model and coding method. *Journal of Cognitive Development, 12*(4), 424–462. https://doi.org/10.1080/15248372.2011.587854

Reese, E., Jack, F., & White, N. (2010). Origins of adolescents' autobiographical memories. *Cognitive Development, 25*, 352–367. https://psycnet.apa.org/doi/10.1016/j.cogdev.2010.08.006

Reese, E., & Robertson, S-J. (2019). Origins of adolescents' earliest memories. *Memory, 27*(1), 79–91. https://doi.org/10.1080/09658211.2018.1512631

Reijula, S., & Hertwig, R. (2022). Self-nudging and the citizen choice architect. *Behavioral Public Policy, 6*(1), 119–149. https://doi.org/10.1017/bpp.2020.5

Richeson, J. (2020, Sept.). Americans are determined to believe in black progress. *The Atlantic*.

Ricour, P. (1992). *Oneself as another*. Chicago, IL: University of Chicago Press.

Ris, E. W. (2015). Grit: A short history of a useful concept. *Journal of Educational Controversy, 10*(1). https://cedar.wwu.edu/jec/vol10/iss1/3

REFERENCES

Roberts, B. W., & DelVecchio, W. F. (2000). The rank-order consistency of personality traits from childhood to old age: A quantitative review of longitudinal studies. *Psychological Bulletin, 126*(1), 3-25. https://psycnet.apa.org/doi/10.1037/0033-2909.126.1.3

Roberts, B. W., & Mroczek, D. (2008). Personality trait change in adulthood. *Current Directions in Psychological Science, 17*(1), 31-35. https://doi.org/10.1111/j.1467-8721.2008.00543.x

Roberts, B. W., & Nickel, L. B. (2021). Personality development across the life course: A neo-socioanalytic perspective. In O. P. John & R. W. Robins (Eds.), *Handbook of personality: Theory and research* (pp. 259-283). New York, NY: Guilford Press.

Roberts, B. W., Walton, K. E., & Viechtbauer, W. (2006). Patterns of mean-level change in personality traits across the life course: A meta-analysis of longitudinal studies. *Psychological Bulletin, 132*(1), 1-25. https://psycnet.apa.org/doi/10.1037/0033-2909.132.1.1

Roberts, B. W., & Wood, D. (2006). Personality development in the context of the neo-socioanalytic model of personality. In D. K. Mroczek & T. D. Little (Eds.), *Handbook of personality development* (pp. 11-39). Mahwah, NJ: Erlbaum.

Roberts, S. O., Bareket-Shavit, C., Dollins, F. A., Goldie, P. D., & Mortenson, E. (2020). Racial inequality in psychological research: Trends of the past and recommendations for the future. *Perspectives on Psychological Science, 15*(6), 1295-1309. https://doi.org/10.1177%2F1745691620927709

Robinson, O. C., Noftle, E. E., Guo, J., Asadi, S., & Zhang, X. (2015). Goals and plans for Big Five personality trait change in young adults. *Journal of Research in Personality, 59*, 31-43. https://psycnet.apa.org/doi/10.1016/j.jrp.2015.08.002

Rogers, L. O. (2018). Who am I, who are we? Erikson and a transactional approach to identity research. *Identity, 18*(4), 284-294. https://psycnet.apa.org/doi/10.1080/15283488.2018.1523728

Rogers, L. O. (2020, November 4). Who am I, who are we? How do children and teens come to understand who they can become? *Psychology Today*. https://www.psychologytoday.com/us/blog/who-am-i-who-are-we/202011/who-am-i-who-are-we

Rogers, L. O., & Heard-Garris, N. (2023). Documenting racial disparities or disrupting racism? A call to center systems of power, privilege, and oppression in psychological and pediatric research. *JAMA Pediatrics, 177*(2), 113-114. https://doi.org/10.1001/jamapediatrics.2022.3862.

Rogers, L. O., Moffitt, U., & Jones, C. M. (2021). *Listening for culture: Using interviews to understand identity in context.* In K. C. McLean (Ed.), *Cultural methods in psychology: Describing and transforming cultures.* New York, NY: Oxford University Press.

Rogers, L. O., Moffitt, U., McLean, K. C., & Syed, M. (2023). Research as resistance: Dismantling the master narrative of good science. *American Psychologist.*

Rogers, L., O., Niwa, E., Y., Chung, K., Yip, T., & Chae, D. (2021). M(ai)cro: Centering the macrosystem in human development. *Human Development, 65*, 70-92. https://doi.org/10.1159/000519630

Rogers, L. O., Rosario, R. J., Padilla, D., & Foo, C. (2021). "[I] t's hard because it's the cops that are killing us for stupid stuff": Racial identity in the sociopolitical context of Black Lives Matter. *Developmental Psychology, 57*(1), 87. https://psycnet.apa.org/doi/10.1037/dev0001130

Rogers, L. O., Versey, H. S., & Cielto, J. (2021). "They're always gonna notice my natural hair": Identity, intersectionality and resistance among Black girls. *Qualitative Psychology.* https://doi.org/10.1037/qup0000208

Rogers, L. O., & Way, N. (2018). Reimagining social and emotional development: Accommodation and resistance to dominant ideologies in the identities and friendships of boys of color. *Human Development, 61,* 311–331. https://doi.org/10.1159/000493378

Rogers, L. O., & Way, N. (2021). Child development in an ideological context: Through the lens of resistance and accommodation. *Child Development Perspectives, 15*(4), 242–248. https://doi.org/10.1111/cdep.12433

Rogoff, B. (2003). *The cultural nature of human development.* New York, NY: Oxford University Press.

Roisman, G. L., Padrón, E., Sroufe, L. A., & Egeland, B. (2002). Earned-secure attachment status in retrospect and prospect. *Child Development, 73*(4), 1204–1219. https://doi.org/10.1111/1467-8624.00467

Rosenthal, R. (1979). The file drawer problem and tolerance for null results. *Psychological Bulletin, 86*(3), 638–641. https://doi.org/10.1037/0033-2909.86.3.638

Rozin, P. (2001). Social psychology and science: Some lessons from Solomon Asch. *Personality and Social Psychology Review, 5*(1), 2–14. https://doi.org/10.1207/S15327957PSPR0501_1

Rucker, J. M., & Richeson, J. A. (2021). Toward an understanding of structural racism: Implications for criminal justice. *Science, 374*(6565), 286–290. https://doi.org/10.1126/science.abj7779

Ruggeri, K., & Folke, T. (2022). Unstandard deviation: The untapped value of positive deviance for reducing inequalities. *Perspectives on Psychological Science, 17*(3), 711–731. https://doi.org/10.1177%2F17456916211017865

Ryff, C. D. (2022). Positive psychology: Looking back and looking forward. *Frontiers in Psychology, 13.* https://doi.org/10.3389/fpsyg.2022.840062

Sales, J. M., Merrill, N. A., & Fivush, R. (2013). Does making meaning make it better? Narrative meaning making and well-being in at-risk African-American adolescent females. *Memory, 21*(1), 97–110. https://doi.org/10.1080/09658211.2012.706614

Salter, P., & Adams, G. (2013). Toward a critical race psychology. *Social and Personality Psychology Compass, 7*(11), 781–793. https://doi.org/10.1111/spc3.12068

Sarbin, T. R. (Ed.). (1986). *Narrative psychology: The storied nature of human conduct.* New York, NY: Praeger.

Saunders, R., Jacobvitz, D., Zaccagnino, M., Beverung, L. M., & Hazen, N. (2011). Pathways to earned-security: The role of alternative support figures. *Attachment and Human Development, 13*(4), 403–420. https://doi.org/10.1080/14616734.2011.584405

Scheel, A. M., Tiokhin, L., Isager, P. M., & Lakens, D. (2021). Why hypothesis testers should spend less time testing hypotheses. *Perspectives on Psychological Science, 16*(4), 744–755. https://doi.org/10.1177/1745691620966795

Schneider, S. L., & Wright, R. C. (2004). Understanding denial in sexual offenders: A review of cognitive and motivational processes to avoid responsibility. *Trauma Violence Abuse, 5*(1), 3–20. https://doi.org/10.1177%2F1524838003259320

REFERENCES

Settles, I. H., Warner, L. R., Buchanan, N. T., & Jones, M. K. (2020). Understanding psychology's resistance to intersectionality theory using a framework of epistemic exclusion and invisibility. *Journal of Social Issues, 76*(4), 796–813. https://doi.org/10.1111/josi.12403

Shiner, R. L., & DeYoung, C. G. (2013). The structure of temperament and personality traits: A developmental perspective. In P. D. Zelazo (Ed.), *The Oxford handbook of developmental psychology, Vol. 2. Self and other* (pp. 113–141). New York, NY: Oxford University Press.

Shirley (no last name given). (2018). Red Lake Band of Ojibwe. Retrieved fromhttps://www.originatives.org/joe-digital-story.

Shonkoff, J. P., & Phillips, D. A. (Eds.). (2000). *From neurons to neighborhoods: The science of early childhood development.* Washington, DC: National Academies Press.

Singer, J. (1997). *Message in a bottle: Stories of men and addiction.* New York, NY: Free Press.

Singer, J., Blagov, P., Berry, M., & Oost, K. (2013). Self-defining memories, scripts, and the life story: Narrative identity in personality and psychotherapy. *Journal of Personality, 81*(6), 569–582. https://doi.org/10.1111/jopy.12005

Skowronski, J. J., Walker, W. R., Henderson, D. X., & Bond, G. D. (2014). The fading affect bias: Its history, its implications, and its future. In J. M. Olson & M. P. Zanna (Eds.), *Advances in experimental social psychology* (Vol. 49, pp. 163–218). New York, NY: Elsevier Academic Press.

Snyder, R. L. (2019). *No visible bruises: What we don't know about domestic violence can kill us.* New York, NY: Elsevier.

Solórzano, D. G., & Yosso, T. J. (2002). Critical race methodology: Counter-storytelling as an analytical framework for education research. *Qualitative Inquiry, 8*(1), 23–44. https://doi.org/10.1177%2F107780040200800103

Southern Poverty Law Center. (2018). Teaching hard history. https://www.splcenter.org/20180131/teaching-hard-history

Spellman, B. A. (2015). A short (personal) future history of Revolution 2.0. *Perspectives on Psychological Science, 10*(6), 886–899. https://doi.org/10.1177%2F1745691615609918

Spencer, M. B. (2017). Privilege and critical race perspectives' intersectional contributions to a systems theory of human development. In N. Budwig, E. Turiel, & P. D. Zelazo (Eds.), *New perspectives on human development* (pp. 287–312). Cambridge, England: Cambridge University Press. https://doi.org/10.1017/CBO9781316282755.016

Spencer, M. B., Dupree, D., & Hartmann, T. (1997). A phenomenological variant of ecological systems theory (PVEST): A self-organization perspective in context. *Development and Psychopathology, 9*(4), 817–833. https://doi.org/10.1017/S0954579497001454

Stevenson, B. (2020). "Just mercy" attorney asks U.S. to reckon with its racist past and present. *Fresh Air.* https://www.npr.org/transcripts/796234496

Stevenson, H. C., & Arrington, E. G. (2009). Racial/ethnic socialization mediates perceived racism and the racial identity of African American adolescents. *Cultural Diversity and Ethnic Minority Psychology, 15*(2), 125–136. https://doi.org/10.1037/a0015500

Stoudt, B. G., Fox, M., & Fine, M. (2012). Contesting privilege with critical participatory action research. *Journal of Social Issues, 68*(1), 178–193. https://doi.org/10.1111/j.1540-4560.2011.01743.x

Sutherland, P., & Chakrabarti, M. (2022). An "invisible epidemic": Survivors of domestic violence on living with traumatic brain injury. *On Point.* https://www.wbur.org/onpoint/2022/01/20/survivors-of-domestic-violence-on-living-with-traumatic-brain-injury

Swann, W. B., Jr. (2012). Self-verification theory. In P. A. M. Van Lange, A. W. Kruglanski, & E. T. Higgins (Eds.), *Handbook of theories of social psychology* (pp. 23–42). Newbury Park, CA: Sage. https://doi.org/10.4135/9781446249222.n27

Sweet, P. L. (2021). *The politics of surviving: How women navigate domestic violence and its aftermath* (1st ed.). Berkeley, CA: University of California Press. https://doi.org/10.2307/j.ctv20dsb3k

Syed, M. (2019, April 15). The open science movement is for all of us. https://doi.org/10.31234/osf.io/cteyb

Syed, M. (2022, July 13). Should we care that we changed the meaning of idiographic? A call for psychology to embrace the original meaning. https://doi.org/10.31234/osf.io/hsp5v

Syed, M., & Azmitia, M. (2010). Narrative and ethnic identity exploration: A longitudinal account of emerging adults' ethnicity-related experiences. *Developmental Psychology, 46*(1), 208–219. https://doi.org/10.1037/a0017825

Syed, M., Azmitia, M., & Cooper, C. R. (2011). Identity and academic success among underrepresented ethnic minorities: An interdisciplinary review and integration. *Journal of Social Issues, 67*(3), 442–468. https://doi.org/10.1111/j.1540-4560.2011.01709.x

Syed, M., & Fish, J. (2018). Revisiting Erik Erikson's legacy on culture, race, and ethnicity. *Identity: An International Journal of Theory and Research, 18*(4), 274–283. https://doi.org/10.1080/15283488.2018.1523729

Syed, M., Juan, M. J. D., & Juang, L. P. (2011). Might the survey be the intervention? Participating in ethnicity-related research as a consciousness-raising experience. *Identity: An International Journal of Theory and Research, 11*(4), 289–310 http://dx.doi.org/10.1080/15283488.2011.613581

Syed, M., & Kathawalla, U-K. (2021). Cultural psychology, diversity, and representation in open science. In K. C. McLean (Ed.), *Cultural methodologies in psychology: Describing and transforming cultures* (pp. 427–454). New York, NY: Oxford University Press.

Syed, M., & McLean, K. C. (2016). Understanding identity integration: Theoretical, methodological, and applied issues. *Journal of Adolescence, 47,* 109–118. https://doi.org/10.1016/j.adolescence.2015.09.005

Syed, M., & McLean, K. C. (2021). Master narrative methodology: A primer for conducting structural-psychological research. *Cultural Diversity and Ethnic Minority Psychology.* https://doi.org/10.1037/cdp0000470

Syed, M., & McLean, K. C. (2022a). Who gets to live the good life? Master narratives, identity, and well-being within a marginalizing society. *Journal of Research in Personality.*

REFERENCES

Syed, M., & Mclean, K. C. (2022b). Disentangling paradigm and method can help bring qualitative research to post-positivist psychology and address the generalizability crisis. *Behavioral and Brain Sciences*, *45*, 58–60. https://doi.org/10.1017/S0140525X21000431

Syed, M., Santos, C., Yoo, H. C., & Juang, L. P. (2018). Invisibility of racial/ethnic minorities in developmental science: Implications for research and institutional practices. *American Psychologist*, *73*(6), 812–826. https://doi.org/10.1037/amp0000294

Tatum, B. (2000). The complexity of identity: "Who am I?" In M. Adams, W. Blumenfeld, H. Hackman, X. Zuniga, & M. Peters (Eds.), *Readings for diversity and social justice: An anthology on racism, sexism, anti-semitism, heterosexism, classism and ableism* (pp. 9–14). New York, NY: Routledge.

Taylor, C. (1989). *Sources of the self: The making of the modern identity*. Cambridge, MA: Harvard University Press.

Tedeschi, R. G., & Calhoun, L. G. (1996). The posttraumatic growth inventory: Measuring the positive legacy of trauma. *Journal of Traumatic Stress*, *9*(3), 455–472. https://doi.org/10.1002/jts.2490090305

Tedeschi, R. G., & Calhoun, L. G. (2004). Posttraumatic growth: Conceptual foundations and empirical evidence. *Psychological Inquiry*, *15*(1), 1–18. https://doi.org/10.1207/s15327965pli1501_01

Teo, T. (2010). What is epistemological violence in the empirical social sciences? *Social and Personality Psychology Compass*, *4*, 295–303. https://doi.org/10.1111/j.1751-9004.2010.00265.x

Thompson, R. A. (2004). Shaping the brains of tomorrow: What developmental science teaches about the importance of investing early in children. https://sedlpubs.faculty.ucdavis.edu/wp-content/uploads/sites/192/2015/03/Thompson2004.pdf

Thorne, A. (2000). Personal memory telling and personality development. *Personality and Social Psychology Review*, *4*(1), 45–56. https://doi.org/10.1207/S15327957PSPR0401_5

Thorne, A., Cutting, L., & Skaw, D. (1998). Young adults' relationship memories and the life story: Examples or essential landmarks? *Narrative Inquiry*, *8*(2), 237–268. https://doi.org/10.1075/ni.8.2.02tho

Thorne, A., McLean, K. C., & Dasbach, A. (2004). When parents' stories go to pot: Telling personal transgressions to teenage kids. In M. W. Pratt & B. H. Fiese (Eds.), *Family stories and the life course: Across time and generations* (pp. 187–209). New York, NY: Erlbaum.

Tocqueville, Alexis de. (1835). *Democracy in America*. New York, NY: G. Dearborn & Co.,

Turner, K., Weststrate, N. M., & McLean, K. C. (2023). Coming Into Queer: A Mixed-Method Exploration of Queer Socialization Experiences Among LGBTQ+ Emerging Adults. *Manuscript Under Review*.

Trinkenreich, B., Britto, R., Gerosa, M. A., & Steinmacher, I. (2022, May). An empirical investigation on the challenges faced by women in the software industry: A case study. In *2022 IEEE/ACM 44th International Conference on Software Engineering: Software Engineering in Society (ICSE-SEIS)* (pp. 24–35). https://doi.org/10.1145/3510458.3513018

Tsosie, R. (2012). Indigenous peoples and epistemic injustice: Science, ethics, and human rights. *Washington Law Review*, 87, 133–1201. https://digitalcommons.law.uw.edu/wlr/vol87/iss4/5

Tuck, E., & Yang, K. W. (Eds.). (2014). *Youth resistance research and theories of change* (1st ed.). London, England: Routledge. https://doi.org/10.4324/9780203585078

Tversky, B., & Marsh, E. J. (2000). Biased retellings of events yield biased memories. *Cognitive Psychology*, 40(1), 1--38. https://doi.org/10.1006/cogp.1999.0720

Umaña-Taylor, A. J., Quintana, S. M., Lee, R. M., Cross, W. E., Jr., Rivas-Drake, D., Schwartz, S. J., . . . Seaton, E. (2014). Ethnic and racial identity during adolescence and into young adulthood: An integrated conceptualization. *Child Development*, 85(1), 21–39. https://doi.org/10.1111/cdev.12196

U.S. Commission on Civil Rights. (2022). *The civil rights implications of cash bail.* https://www.usccr.gov/files/2022-01/USCCR-Bail-Reform-Report-01-20-22.pdf

Vazire, S. (2018). Implications of the credibility revolution for productivity, creativity, and progress. *Perspectives on Psychological Science*, 13(4), 411–417. https://doi.org/10.1177/1745691617751884

Vesey, B. M., Martinez, D. J., & Christina, J. (2009). Identity transformation and offender change. In B. M. Veysey, J. Christian, & D. J. Martinez (Eds.), *How offenders transform their lives* (pp. 1–11). Cullompton, Devon, UK: Culmcott House.

Victor, J., & Waldram, J. (2015). Moral habilitation and the new normal: Sexual offender narratives of posttreatment community integration. In L. Presser & S. Sandberg (Eds.), *Narrative criminology: Understanding stories of crime* (pp. 96–122). New York, NY: New York University Press. https://doi.org/10.18574/nyu/9781479876778.003.0005

Vizenor, G. (Ed.). (2008). *Survivance: Narratives of Native presence.* Lincoln, NE: University of Nebraska Press.

Wagner, J., Orth, U., Bleidorn, W., Hopwood, C. J., & Kandler, C. (2020). Toward an integrative model of sources of personality stability and change. *Current Directions in Psychological Science*, 29(5), 438–444. https://doi.org/10.1177/0963721420924751

Wainryb, C. (2011). "And so they ordered me to kill a person": Conceptualizing the impacts of child soldiering on the development of moral agency. *Human Development*, 54(5), 273–300. https://www.jstor.org/stable/26765014

Waters, T. E. A., Köber, C., Raby, K. L., Habermas, T., & Fivush, R. (2019). Consistency and stability of narrative coherence: An examination of personal narrative as a domain of adult personality. *Journal of Personality*, 87(2), 151–162. https://doi.org/10.1111/jopy.12377

Weis, L., & Fine, M. (2012). Critical bifocality and circuits of privilege: Expanding critical ethnographic theory and design. *Harvard Educational Review*, 82(2), 173–201. https://doi.org/10.17763/haer.82.2.v1jx34n441532242

Weisner, T. S. (2002). Ecocultural understanding of children's developmental pathways. *Human Development*, 45(4), 275–281.

Weststrate, N. M. (2021). Using life story methods to illuminate cultural-historical dimensions of LGBTQ+ identity development across generations. In *Cultural methods in psychology: Describing and transforming cultures* (pp. 3–44). New York, NY: Oxford University Press.

Weststrate, N. M., & McLean, K. C. (2010). The rise and fall of gay: A cultural-historical approach to gay identity development. *Memory, 18*(2), 225–240. https://psycnet.apa.org/doi/10.1080/09658210903153923

Weststrate, N. M., & McLean, K. C. (2022). Protest, panic, policy, and parades: Memory for cultural-historical events and psychosocial identity in the LGBTQ+ community. *Psychology of Sexual Orientation and Gender Diversity*, Advance online publication. https://doi.org/10.1037/sgd0000582.

Weststrate, N. M., Turner, K., & McLean, K. C. (2023). Intergenerational storytelling as a developmental resource in the LGBTQ+ community. *Journal of Homosexuality*, 1–26. Advance online publication. https://doi.org/10.1080/00918369.2023.2202295.

Williamson, J., & Serna, K. (2018). Reconsidering forced labels: Outcomes of sexual assault survivors versus victims (and those who choose neither). *Violence Against Women, 24*(6), 668–683. https://doi.org/10.1177/1077801217711268

Wrzus, C., & Roberts, B. W. (2017). Processes of personality development in adulthood: The TESSERA framework. *Personality and Social Psychology Review, 21*(3), 253–277. https://doi.org/10.1177/1088868316652279

Yakushko, O. (2019). *Scientific Pollyannaism: From inquisition to positive psychology*. London: Palgrave Macmillan. https://doi.org/10.1007/978-3-030-15982-5

Yarkoni, T. (2022). The generalizability crisis. *Behavioral and Brain Sciences, 45*. https://doi.org/10.1017/S0140525X20001685

Yarkoni, T., & Westfall, J. (2017). Choosing prediction over explanation in psychology: Lessons from machine learning. *Perspectives on Psychological Science, 12*(6), 1100–1122. https://doi.org/10.1177/1745691617693393

Yee, A. M., Mazumder, P. K., Dong, F., & Neeki, M. M. (2020). Impact of healthcare access disparities on initial diagnosis of breast cancer in the emergency department. *Cureus, 12*(8), e10027. https://doi.org/10.7759/cureus.10027

INDEX

For the benefit of digital users, indexed terms that span two pages (e.g., 52–53) may, on occasion, appear on only one of those pages.

Tables are indicated by *t* following the page number

academe, complicity of, in perpetuation of master narratives, 34–36
academic psychology, 29–30
accommodation, learning process, 112–13
addiction, cycles of, 32
Adichie, Chimamanda Ngozi, 33–34, 124
Adler, Jon
   on acquired disability, 97
   on disability in adulthood, 89–90, 92
   on repeated narratives, 88
agency
   biases shaping focus on, 132–33
   idea of, 111
   maintaining perception of, 29–30
   master narratives and, 9, 110
   overemphasized personal control and, 9
   personal, 110
   power of, 110–11
   resistance as form of, 12–13
   resistance as particular kind of, 112–13
Alabama, Confederate Memorial Day, 57
Alcoholics Anonymous, 58–59, 100
Alger, Horatio, narrative, 22
alternative narratives
   dismissing, 16–17
   master and, 6
   term, 112
American culture
   individuals controlling own destinies, 3
   mainstream, 20
   radical individualism in, 4
American Dream, 58–59, 61
American exceptionalism, 23
American Psychological Association, 73–74
Amherst, Jeffrey, 46–47
Amherst College, 46–47
assimilation, learning process, 112–13
atonement
   identity change and, 101
   as pathway to change, 101
   redemption in form of, 97–98
attachment representation
   change in self-reported, 72–73
   "earned secure" person, 71–72
   expectation of stability in, 71–72
   personality development, 70–73
autobiographical reasoning, idea of, 11, 34–35

biases
   acknowledging own, 36
   shaping individual agency, 132–33
   transparency in, 138–39
Big Five personality traits, 65–66
   agreeableness, personality trait, 65–66

Big Five personality traits (*cont.*)
   conscientiousness, personality trait, 65–66
   extraversion/Introversion, personality trait, 65–66
   neuroticism/Emotional Stability, personality trait, 65–66
   openness to Experience, personality trait, 65–66
Black Lives Matter (BLM) movement, 120, 121
Booker, Jordan, 135
Branson, Richard, 3
Brown, Michael, murder of, 24, 120
Bryant, Kobe, public story, 103–4
Buffalo Soldiers, 32
Bush, George, Sr., Richards on, 110–11
Butler, The (movie), 22–23

canalization, concept of, 70–71
capitalism, 16
change
   concept of, 49
   cultural stories as obstacles to, 57–62
   defining and measuring, 49–50
   difficulty of, 54–62
   ethics of, 104–8
   expecting, in stories, 54
   forcing ourselves to start fresh, 133–34
   importance of prediction and control, 55–56
   intervention question, 131–32
   obstacles to, 62
   people and, 10
   person and society, 18
   possibility of, 49–50
   possibility of personality, 69–70
   rigidity of culture and challenge of, 22–26
   scientific responsibility for, 15–18
   See also personal change; scientific responsibility for change; transgressions
character skills, 15

Children of the Setting Sun Productions (CSSP), 117
Clinton, Bill, public story, 103–4
Coast Salish Tribes, Native Americans, 117, 118
coauthored self, 9–10
Cobb, Jelani
   on Brown's murder, 24
   history of Kerner Commission, 57
   The New York Review of Books, 23
cognitive development, Piaget's conception of, 86
collective reflection, 132
Confederate Memorial Day, Alabama, 57
Constitution, 4
   individual rights in, 6–7
consumerism, promising change, 28
contexts, identity integration through, 37, 40–41
COVID-19, behavioral change and, 70
criminal justice, resistance in, 113
critical race theory, resistance in, 113
cultural group, identity integration through, 37, 41–43
culture
   conceptions of, 21
   definition of, 20
   redemption narratives and, 131–32
   rigidity of, and challenge of change, 22–26
   role of, 17–18
   story of, 11
   values and, 20–21, 22
Cushman, Philip
   conceptions of self, 26–27
   empty self and, 27–34
   Why the Self Is Empty, 26–27

developmental resources
   story transmission within marginalized communities as, 119–20
   Weststrate on stories as, 60
diversity and representation, psychology, 132
domestic violence, 106, 108

INDEX

education
  agentic and redemptive story of, 111–12
  campaign "The Road to Resilience," 73–74
  resistance in, 113
  structural support of system, 25
epistemic injustice, Fricker on, 119–20
Equal Justice Initiative, 57
Erikson, Erik, 60
  concept of identity integration, 38
  on Native Americans, 38, 60
  temporal discontinuity, 38
  working with veterans, 40
ethic of care, respecting stories and storytellers, 136
experimental design, observation and description of stories, 133–34

feminist studies, resistance in, 113
Fine, Michelle, concept of strong objectivity, 138
Fish, Jill, 46, 114–16, 118
Fivush, Robyn, 11
Floyd, George, murder of, 23–24
42 (movie), 22–23
Fraley, Chris
  change in self-reported attachment, 72–73
  concept of canalization, 70–71
Frankl, Viktor E., 4
Fricker, Miranda, epistemic injustice, 119–20

Green Book (movie), 22–23

Hakken, Janice, *Hard Knocks*, 108
Hammack, Phil, 11
Helms, Janet, model for white racial identity development, 126
hermeneutical injustice, Fricker on, 119–20
homelessness, family experiencing, 32
Hudson, Nate, data on volitional trait change, 69

identities
  defining, 9–10, 37
  formation of, 37–38
  positions of power and privilege, 13
  possibility of changing one's, 65, 76
  storying, 47–54
  storytelling as process of development of, 98–99
  See also identity integration; narrative identity; storying identity
identity change
  atonement and, 101
  change by degrees, 86–89
  context of, 92–94
  master narrative of redemption, 91–92, 93–94
  opportunity for, 87–88
  potential, 90
  reasoning about, 90–91
  seismic change, 89–92
  two-degrees trajectory, 86–87
  See also narrative identity
identity domains, defining ourselves in, 40
identity integration, 37
  across contexts, 40–41
  challenges of identity work for those on margins, 44–45
  concept of, 38
  cultural belonging and, 41–43
  devaluing or denial of central parts of self, 45
  navigating, within mainstream culture, 45
  need for systemic change for all, 46–47
  personal and collective responsibility for work of, 43–47
  through time, 38–39
Identity Pathways Project, Lilgendahl of, 40–41
individual(s), 19–20
  psychology of, 35–36
  rights in Constitution, 6–7
  understanding characteristics of, 18
  unique power of, 4
injustice
  hermeneutical, 119–20
  testimonial, 119–20

Johnson, Lyndon, Kerner Commission Report, 23

Kavanaugh, Brent, public story, 103–4
Kerner Commission Report, 23–24, 25, 57
   intentions behind, 59–60

Law and Order (television show), 25
legal system, structural support, 25
LGBTQ+ youth
   families and communities raising, 118–19
   identity integration, 45
   identity work, 44–45
   queer elders and, 136–37
   survey data of, 137
   access to books by, 24–25
   cultivation of resistance stories, 118–19
Lilgendahl, Jennifer Pals, Identity Pathways Project, 40–41

Manifest Destiny, 4, 6
Martin Luther King Day, 57
Maslow, Abraham, 4
master narratives, 5, 29–30
   addiction and impact on community, 58–60
   agency and, 110
   alternative narratives and, 6
   American values, 25–26
   complicity of academe in perpetuation of, 34–36
   cultural ideology of personal growth, 31
   dark side to, 5
   maintaining hierarchies of power, 22–23
   narrative identity, 50, 53–54
   origin of United States, 6
   personal responsibility for growth and change, 7–8
   power in, 13–14, 35
   power of the individual, 5
   race, 57–59
   redemption, 31–32, 91–92, 93–94
   refusing, repudiation and contesting of, 113
   structure and system, 7
   telling resistance stories to dismantle, 113
   Vygotskian approach, 21
maturity principle, Roberts, 67, 79
Message in a Bottle (Singer), 58–59
money bail system, 25
moral agency, definition, 104–5
MSNBC, choosing to watch, 55–56

narrative identity
   authenticity of atonement story, 101–2
   change by degrees, 86–89
   context of identity change, 92–94
   developmental approaches to, 51–53, 131
   intra-individual variability in, 80–81
   master narrative approaches to, 53–54
   motive in memory narratives, 79
   personality approaches to, 50–51
   rank-order stability in narration, 79–80
   repeated narration, 77
   self-event connections, 80
   storytelling, 8
   See also repeated narration
Native Americans
   challenging invisibility of, 117
   challenging master narratives of, 114–15, 116, 118
   Children of the Setting Sun Productions, 117
   Coast Salish Tribes, 117, 118
   Erikson's learning from, 38, 60
   OrigiNatives digital storytelling project, 115–16
   Salmon People Project, 117, 118
neoliberalism, 16
Neo-Socioanalytic Model of Personality, Roberts, 67

Obama, Barack, electoral victory of, 22–23
O'Brien, Tim
   on horrors of war, 39
   The Things They Carried, 39
On Point podcast, 92–93

INDEX

ontological security
  importance of prediction and control, 55–56
  phenomenon, 56
openness and replicability, psychology, 132
optimism, 18
OrigiNatives, digital storytelling project, 115–17

participatory action research, methodology of, 137–38
Pasupathi, Monisha, 11
patriarchy, white supremacy and, 13, 28–29
perpetrators
  authenticity of atonement story, 101–2
  comparing stories of victim and, 104–8
  as "good boys" or from "good families," 103
  pressure for change on incarcerated, 102–3
  privilege of, based on social class, 103
  public stories of atonement, 103–4
  society side of things and, 104
  storytelling as healing, 101
  transgression stories from, 100–2
  victims and, 104
  Weinstein as, 103–4
  See also transgressions
personal autonomy, 9
personal change, 3
  study of stories and, 8–15
personal control, overemphasis, 9
personal growth
  cultural press for stories of, 36
  emphasis on change and, 61
  ideology of, 31
  infatuation with redemption and, 132–33
personality development, 65
  character strengths, 74
  maturity principle, 67
  mean-level change, 66, 79
  methodological challenges, 75–76
  possibility of change, 69–70
  posttraumatic growth, 73–75
  rank-order stability, 66, 79–80
  second level of, 66

self-nudges, 69
trait and behavior change, 69–70
trait change, 66–70
volitional trait change, 68–69
p-hacking, 75–76
Piaget, Jean, conception of cognitive development, 86
Politics of Surviving, The (Sweet), 106
posttraumatic growth, 19–20
  character strengths, 74
  concept of, 34, 73–74
  concept of "The Positive Legacies of Trauma," 30–31
  contemporary examples of, 30–34
posttraumatic stress disorder (PTSD), 106
poverty
  personal responsibility and, 25
power
  stories maintaining hierarchy of, 22–23
  structures in psychology, 132

racial identities
  combining personal, interpersonal, and sociopolitical contexts, 122–24
  development of, 122
  importance of, 120–21
  model for white, development, 126
  privilege of, 126–27
  resistance and "The Talk," 122–23, 126–27
racism
  master narrative in United States, 22–23
  movies on pain and struggle of, 22–23
radical intentionality, Rogers on, 138–39
redemption
  Alcoholics Anonymous, 100
  concept of, 31–32, 34
  cultural press for, 32
  culture and full story, 131–32
  infatuation with personal growth and, 132–33
  master narratives of, 91–92, 93–94
  power of, 36
  press for and love of, 33
  survivors and redemptive narrative, 106–7
  twelve-step program, 101

repeated narration
  change of how in storytelling over time, 79–81
  change of telling specific events over time, 81–86
  event repetition, 82t
  repetition as exploration, 84
  repetition as importance, 84–85
  repetition as stagnation, 83–84
  repetition signals culturally valued stories, 85–86
  role of master narratives in, 85
  two-degrees-type trajectory of, 86–87, 88
  See also narrative identity
resilience, 15, 16
resistance
  broadening the responsibility for, 125–27
  collective work of, 113
  component of human development, 114
  definition of, 112, 114
  as developmental process, 113–14
  message of, for liberation, 122–23
  as particular kind of agency, 112–13
  protest and, 26
  story as place to cultivate, 60–61
resistance stories
  cultivation of, 119
  interpersonal contexts for, 114–20
  intertwining of personal, interpersonal and sociopolitical contexts, 122–25
  sociopolitical contexts of, 120–22
  within LGBTQ+ community, 118–19
restorative justice, storytelling as healing, 101
Richards, Ann, on George Bush Sr., 110–11
"Road to Resilience, The," American Psychological Association campaign, 73–74
Robbins, Tony, 3, 10
Roberts, Brent
  maturity principle, 67, 79
  mean-level change, 67–68
  Neo-Socioanalytic Model of Personality, 67
  self-continuity principle, 74

Robinson, Jackie, success of, 23
Roethlisberger, Ben, public story, 103–4
Rogers, Onnie, 12
  radical intentionality of efforts, 138–39

Salmon People Project, Native Americans, 117, 118
scientific polyannaism, 34
scientific responsibility for change
  experimental design, 133–34
  focus on resilience, 15–16
  interpretations and purpose, 134
  listening to stories from more people, 134
  proposals in scientific practices, 133–38
  psychological turn, 16–17
  psychology, 16, 17–18
  respecting the stories and storytellers, 136–37
  systems and structures in, 15–16, 17–18, 134
  See also change
self
  Cushman's argument of empty, 27–34
  definition of, 26–27
  ideology defining as, 27–28
  preservation of, 99
  rational self-domination, 27–28
self-actualization, vision of, 67
self-continuity principle, Roberts, 74
self-control, 15
self-defining memories, 34–35
self-made man, notion of, 4
self-nudges, personality development, 69
self-reflection, 132
sexual identities
  cultural expectations leading to silence and hiding, 42–43
  marginalization of minoritized, 42
silence, sexual identities and, 42–43
Simpson, OJ, public story, 103–4
Singer, Jefferson, 56, 60
  on addiction and stories, 58–60
1619 Project, banning of, 24–25
social media, algorithms of, 55–56
Southern Poverty Law Center, 25

Spencer, Margaret Beale
  on justifying identities, 125–26
  on reflection and self-examination, 126
status quo, 26
  challenge to, 27
Stevenson, Bryan, on narrative about race, 57–58, 59
storying identity, 47–54
  developmental approaches to narrative identity, 51–53
  master narrative approaches to narrative identity, 53–54
  meaning of story, 48–49
  narration, role of others and possibility of change, 49–50
  personality approaches to narrative identity, 50–51
storytelling
  agency in, 9
  changing narratives, 131–32
  comparing victim and perpetrator, 104–8
  hard work in getting into graduate school, 111–12
  narrative identities, 8
  narrative reconstruction of, 108–9
  personal, interpersonal and sociopolitical contexts of, 122–23
  process of, 98–99
  purpose of, 47–48
  restorative justice, 101
strong objectivity
  concept of, 138
  reflexivity or, 138
Supplemental Nutrition Assistance Program, 69
survivance, Vizenor term, 115
survivor(s)
  identity labor, 106
  redemptive narrative and, 106–7
  victims and, of violence, 14, 106–7
Sweet, Paige, 106
Syed, Moin, 11
  on biographical master narratives, 85
  on culture, 22

systemic inequality, 14–15
systems
  deriving success from, 112
  designing, for success, 110–11
  role of, 17–18
  support of, 17
systems and structure
  moving from persons to, 9–15
  scientific responsibility for change, 15–16, 17–18, 134

Taylor, Charles, on "orientation towards the good," 98
testimonial injustice, 119–20
Things They Carried, The (O'Brien), 39
Thomas, Clarence, public story, 103–4
Thorne, Avril, 10–11
time, identity integration through, 37, 38–39
transgressions
  comparing victim and perpetrator stories, 104–8
  ethics of change, 104–8
  fundamental change and, 99–104
  involving perpetrator and victim, 97–98
  motivation for change, 97–98
  narrative reconstruction after, 108–9
  pathways for managing, 98–99
  preservation of self, 99
  societal implications of stories, 102–4
  stories from perpetrator perspective, 100–2
trauma(s)
  concept of positive legacies of, 30–31
  redemptive stories, 106–7
traumatic brain injury (TBI), invisible epidemic of, 92–93
Trump, Donald, public story, 103–4
Turner, Kit
  research on LGBTQ+ youth, 136–37

United States
  American values, 25–26
  master narrative of, 22–23, 25–26
  master narrative of origin, 6
  U.S. Commission on Civil Rights, 25

victim(s)
  comparing stories of perpetrators and, 104–8
  denying reality of, 107
  experiences of, 107
  interpersonal violence, 106–7
  perception of, 107
  of violence, 14, 106–7
  See also transgressions
Vietnam War, O'Brien on, 39
violence
  colonizing, 38
  domestic, 106, 108
  enslavement and, 57–58
  gender- and race-based, 28–29
  interpersonal, 92–93, 97–98, 103–4, 106–7
  perception of, 107
  problem of, 108
  racial, 122–23
  sexual, 101
  state, 23–24
  survivors and victims of, 14, 106–7
Vizenor, Gerald, term 'survivance', 115
volitional trait change, 97
  sources of data on, 69
  term, 68

Weinstein, Harvey, as perpetrator of privilege, 103–4
Weststrate, Nic
  on 'developmental resource' as equity issue, 119–20
  LGBTQ+ community and access to stories, 118–19
  stories as developmental resources, 60
white supremacy, patriarchy and, 13, 28–29
Why the Self Is Empty (Cushman), 26–27
Winfrey, Oprah, 3, 4
World War II, 32, 38, 60